MORE
playful Precut QUILTS

Amand

15 NEW PROJECTS
with Blocks to Mix & Match

stashBOOKS.

an imprint of C&T Publishing

Text copyright © 2023 by Amanda Niederhauser

Photography and artwork copyright © 2023 by
C&T Publishing, Inc.

Publisher: Amy Barrett-Daffin

Creative Director: Gailen Runge

Senior Editor: Roxane Cerda

Editor: Gailen Runge

Technical Editors: Del Walker and Helen Frost

Cover/Book Designer: April Mostek

Production Coordinator: Zinnia Heinzmann

Illustrator: Mary E. Flynn

Photography by Kim Fillmore Photography, unless
otherwise noted

Published by Stash Books, an imprint of C&T Publishing, Inc.,
P.O. Box 1456, Lafayette, CA 94549

Library of Congress Cataloging-in-Publication Data
Names: Niederhauser, Amanda, 1974- author.
Title: More playful precut quilts : 15 projects with blocks
  to mix & match / Amanda Niederhauser.
Description: Lafayette, CA : Stash Books, an imprint of
  C&T Publishing, Inc., [2023] | Summary: "Readers loved
  Amanda Niederhauser's Playful Precut Quilts and with
  this new volume, they will receive 15 more inspiring
  quilt projects all made with 12" blocks. The blocks can
  be mixed and matched across all of the quilts in both
  this new book and her first book for endless creativity"--
  Provided by publisher.
Identifiers: LCCN 2022061390 | ISBN 9781644033371
  (trade paperback) | ISBN 9781644033388 (ebook)
Subjects: LCSH: Patchwork--Patterns. | Quilting-
  -Patterns.
Classification: LCC TT835 .N4949 2023 | DDC
  746.46/041--dc23/eng/20230203
LC record available at https://lccn.loc.gov/2022061390

Printed in China

10 9 8 7 6 5 4 3 2 1

Dedication

To David, Ella, Ryan, and Sally, my amazing family that I love and adore. You have all supported me in my quilting journey. You have put up with a messy house, fending for yourselves in the kitchen, and wearing dirty clothes on occasion. You have held up quilts for photos and videoed endless Instagram reels all while not making fun of me. You are my world.

To all my quilty friends. You are my people! You've been so supportive and you've cheered me on every step of the way! Even when I post way too many cat videos. ☺

To my Jesus. 1 Corinthians 15:10 "But by the grace of God I am what I am." He has been with me every step of the way. Anything I've done or created that is good comes from Him. All glory to His name!

Acknowledgements

A special thanks to my friends at Riley Blake Designs. Thank you for welcoming me into your family. I love our relationship and you've given me so many opportunities to grow and become. Thank you!

Thank you to Hobbs Bonded Fibers for graciously letting me use your batting in my quilts. It's my favorite!

Thank you to Oliso for always sharing your newest irons with me.

Thank you to my darling quilter, Kaylene Parry, who quilts all my quilts and is happy to accommodate my crazy deadlines.

Thank you to my talented photographer, Kim Fillmore, who has been amazing to work with and captured the quilts in this book so well.

A special thanks to C&T Publishing for being so fabulous to work with, for helping me through this process, and for letting me share my quilts with the world.

Contents

projects 10

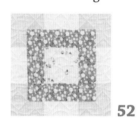

12

20

26

32

40

46

52

58

64

74

80

86

94

98

106

Introduction

Who loves quilts? I do! I do! As quilters we are always looking for our next favorite pattern or our next favorite fabric collection. So much of quilting is gathering items with the hope of making something in the future. We collect piles of books and magazines and we would never disclose to anyone unless under oath how much fabric we actually have. I love this about quilters. We have great anticipation for quilts to come in our future and we get so excited for the process. I wanted to write a book that captures some of this hope that we as quilters have; something to look forward to that brings joy.

More Playful Precut Quilts brings you 15 brand new quilt projects all using 12˝ quilt blocks and fabric precuts. The styles and themes of these quilts cover all seasons and all décor. From strawberries to cats, from summer to Christmas, I wanted to write patterns that would appeal to everyone. This book goes hand in hand with my first book, *Playful Precut Quilts*. Since all the quilt projects use 12˝ blocks, you can take blocks from either book and mix them up and change things around.

I didn't want a book that makes you feel like you must do exactly what I did. Rather, I want you to feel creative and inspired to take my pattern and make it your own through color, fabric, and placement. I want *More Playful Precut Quilts* to be the book you grab when you don't know what to make with that new fat quarter bundle you just purchased. I want this book to inspire hope in you for new quilting possibilities. I can't wait to see what you make!

block diagrams

I love that all the blocks in this book are 12˝, which means you can interchange them and be totally creative! As a helpful tool, I have included a Block Diagram for each of the quilt blocks. The Block Diagram shows the placement and cutting measurements for each piece in the block. This is useful when you are making only a few blocks. The last few chapters of this book include instructions for making a one-block pillow, a four-block table runner, and a nine-block quilt; you get to choose the blocks. Following the Block Diagrams will make sewing these a snap!

Precuts
A QUILTER'S BEST FRIEND

I find myself shopping at quilt shops most often when I don't have a specific project in mind. I go to be inspired, to see what's new, or because I'm on vacation. It's often hard to narrow down my purchase so I gravitate to precuts. I can coordinate a stack of fat quarters in a snap or grab a precise bundle of 5″ squares. I always make sure to choose coordinating yardage for a border or binding at the very least. If a pattern calls for precut squares or strips you can always cut them from yardage yourself.

5″ × 5″ Squares

Bundles of 5″ squares are often called *Charm Packs* or *5″ Stackers*. Within each bundle are a wide variety of fabrics, usually within a specific fabric line. You get a little taste of each fabric without having to purchase yardage.

2½″ × Width of Fabric Strips

Another handy invention is the precut strip bundle. These strips are sometimes referred to as *Jelly Rolls* or *Rolie Polies*. They measure 2½″ × the width of the fabric which is about 42″ long. These are great for strip piecing, log cabin style quilts, and can be cut to a wide range of sizes.

10″ × 10″ Squares

Bundles of 10″ squares are often called *Layer Cakes* or *10″ Stackers*. They have the same variety as 5″ bundles, only they are larger. These larger pieces allow even more versatility!

Fat Quarters

Because a wider piece of fabric is often better than a skinny piece of fabric, quilters invented the fat quarter. A fat quarter measures 18″ × 21″. It's still a quarter yard of fabric, just the fat way. Quilt shops will often cut them upon request. They are a great way to add to your stash when you're not sure what you are going to make. You can always cut them down to 5″ squares, 10″ squares or 2½″ strips as a pattern requires.

Fat Eighths

Fat Eighths are just like fat quarters only with an eighth yard of fabric measuring 9″ × 21″. You'd be surprised what you can make with these and they are a great choice if you want a bundle of fabric but aren't sure what to make.

Scraps

To scrap or not to scrap! If you cut your scraps into precut sizes, you'll be more likely to use them and not waste them. Otherwise you are left with a pile of wrinkly fabrics in all different sizes. Cut your remnants of fabric into 5″ or 10″ squares and 2½″ strips. This makes using scraps so easy.

abbreviations

Width Of Fabric (WOF)

Quilting fabrics usually measure about 42″ wide. All measurements in this book are based on 40″ wide fabric to make sure you have enough since fabrics will vary. Width of fabric is abbreviated in this book as *WOF*.

Width of Fat Quarter (WOFQ)

Fat quarters typically measure 18″ × 21″. In this book, the width of a fat quarter is considered 21″ and abbreviated *WOFQ*.

Right Sides Together (RST)

The seams in this book are sewn with "right sides together". This means the printed sides of the fabric, or the right sides of the fabric are facing each other. Right Sides Together can be abbreviated as *RST*.

Fabric Volume

When talking about fabric, *low volume* and *high volume* refer to the pattern or design and how it reads when mixed with other fabrics. Several projects in this book suggest purchasing either low-volume fabric or high-

volume fabric to achieve the look of the featured quilt.

Low-Volume Fabric

Low-volume fabric pops up often in the quilting community and refers to fabric that is in the cream/white/neutral family. The fabric may have a small design or print but it reads neutral. If you're not sure if your fabric is low volume, place it with the fabrics you are considering and take a step back to look. From a distance it should look neutral.

High-Volume Fabric

High-volume fabric is the opposite of low-volume fabric; these fabrics are full of color and can be solid or patterned.

projects

sunflower garden

When my children were young, we lived near a real pumpkin patch—complete with corn maze, train rides, and a hillside full of sunflowers. The community would make all kinds of scarecrows and put them in the sunflower fields. We would walk through the sunflowers and pick out our favorite scarecrow. This quilt has all the feels of fall. Sort your fabrics into yellow, gold, light brown and dark brown color selections to make these blocks look like real sunflowers!

materials

10˝ × 10˝ PRECUT SQUARES: 1 pack including a minimum of the following:

- 13 light yellow squares
- 13 gold squares
- 13 light brown squares
- 4 dark brown squares

MEDIUM BROWN: ¾ yard for sashing

YELLOW: ¼ yard for sashing

WHITE SOLID: 5 yards for blocks, sashing, and setting triangles

YELLOW PRINT: 1¼ yards for border

BINDING: ¾ yard

BACKING: 7¾ yards

cutting

Precut Squares

- From each of the 13 light yellow 10″ squares, cut 8 squares 3″ × 3″.

- From each of the 13 gold 10″ squares, cut:

  4 squares 3″ × 3″, draw a diagonal line on the wrong side of each

  4 squares 2½″ × 2½″

- From each of the 13 light brown 10″ squares, cut:

  4 squares 3″ × 3″

  4 squares 1½″ × 1½″, draw a diagonal line on the wrong side of each

- From each of the 4 dark brown 10″ squares, cut 4 squares 4½″ × 4½″.

White solid

- Cut 4 strips 2½″ × WOF, subcut into 52 squares 2½″ × 2½″.

- Cut 8 strips 3″ × WOF, subcut into 104 squares 3″ × 3″.

- Cut 4 strips 12½″ × WOF, subcut into 72 rectangles 12½″ × 2″.

- Cut 2 strips 5″ × WOF, subcut into 40 rectangles 5″ × 2″.

- Cut 3 strips 2″ × WOF, set 2 strips aside. Cut the third strip into 6 rectangles 5″ × 2″ and 6 squares 2″ × 2″ for sashing.

- Cut 2 strips 25″ × WOF, subcut into 2 squares 25″ × 25″. Cut each square twice diagonally into quarters making 8 side triangles.

- Cut 1 strip 16½″ × WOF, subcut into 2 squares 16½″. Cut each square in half once diagonally making 4 corner triangles.

Medium brown

- Cut 2 strips 12½″ × WOF, subcut into 36 rectangles 12½″ × 2″.

Yellow

- Cut 2 strips 2″ × WOF, set 1 strip aside. Cut the second strip into 3 squares 2″ × 2″.

Yellow print

- Cut 8 strips 5″ × WOF, sew strips lengthwise together in pairs. Subcut into 2 side borders 77″ × 5″ and 2 top and bottom borders 86″ × 5″. (Wait to cut until quilt top is made and measured.)

Binding

- Cut 9 strips 2½″ × WOF.

Making the Sunflower Block

All seams are ¼″ unless otherwise noted. Follow the pressing arrows shown in the illustrations.

Block Diagram

A: 2½″ × 2½″   C: 1½″ × 1½″
B: 3″ × 3″   D: 4½″ × 4½″

TIP After cutting the fabric it's helpful to sort them into block piles. Choose the yellow, gold, light brown and dark brown fabrics you want in each block and make 13 piles. This will make putting the blocks together easier.

1. Gather 8 matching light yellow 3″ squares and 8 white 3″ squares. Draw a diagonal line on the wrong side of each white square. Pair a yellow square with a white square. Refer to Making Two Half-Square triangles (page 108) for more information on the technique. Make 16 HSTs. Square up the HSTs to measure 2½″ × 2½″. **A**

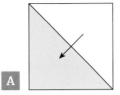

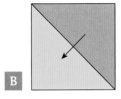

2. Gather 4 gold 3″ squares and 4 light brown 3″ squares. Using the same technique make 8 HSTs. Square up to measure 2½″ × 2½″. **B**

3. Gather 1 dark brown center 4½″ square and 4 light brown 1½″ squares. Position a light brown square in each corner of the dark brown square. Sew on the diagonal line. Trim ¼″ away from the seam and press. **C**

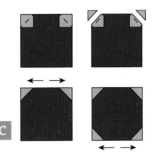

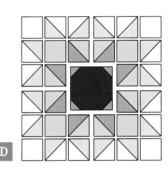

Lay Out the Block

1. Using the 16 yellow/white HSTs, the 8 gold/light brown HSTs, the center dark brown square, 4 white 2½″ squares, and 4 gold 2½″ squares lay out the block. **D**

2. Sew the side HSTs together.

3. Sew to the center square. **E**

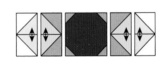

4. Sew the top 2 rows together.

5. Sew the bottom 2 rows. **F**

6. Sew the top 2 rows to the center unit.

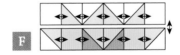

7. Sew the bottom 2 rows to the center unit. The block measures 12½″ at this point. **G**

8. Repeat making 13 Sunflower Blocks total.

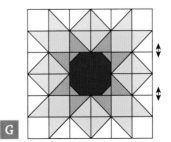

Making the Sashing

1. Gather 2 white 2″ × 12½″ rectangles and 1 medium brown 2″ × 12½″ rectangle. Sew a white rectangle to both sides of a medium brown rectangle lengthwise. Press.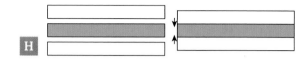

2. Repeat to make 36 sashing rectangle units.

3. Gather the 2 white 2″ × WOF strips and the 1 yellow 2″ × WOF strip. Sew a white strip to both sides of a yellow strip lengthwise. Press.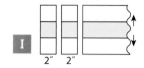

6. Cut the strip unit at 2″ increments. Cut 20 yellow/white square units.

You will need 23 total so gather the 6 white 2″ squares and the 3 yellow 2″ squares. Sew a white 2″ square to both sides of the yellow 2″ square. Press. Make 3 units for a total of 23 yellow/white square units.

7. Gather the 46 white rectangles 2″ × 5″. Sew a rectangle to the top and bottom of the yellow/white square units to make 23 sashing corner units. Corner units measure 5″ × 5″ at this point.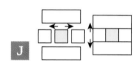

> **TIP** When making a quilt that is set on point, you sew the quilt together diagonally. There are side setting triangles and corner triangles. Be careful not to stretch them while ironing as they have a lot of give. Consider using a light starch to keep them stable. Don't worry if there is excess fabric when putting the quilt together. The whole quilt will get squared up at the end.

Assembling the Quilt

1. Lay out the 13 Sunflower blocks, the sashing rectangles and squares according to the quilt layout diagram. Position the side setting triangles cut from the 25″ square and corner setting triangles cut from the 16½″ squares as pictured. **K**

2. Sew the quilt together in diagonal rows making sure to sew them in the correct order.

Begin by sewing the sashing rows. Press toward the sashing rectangles.

Sew the block rows. Press toward the sashing rectangles.

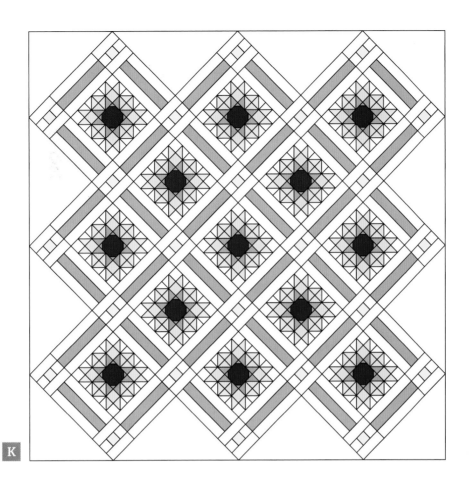

K

3. Join the first block row and the top sashing row. Press. L

4. Sew a triangle to both ends of this row unit, making sure to align the bottom edges. There will be excess fabric at the top. M

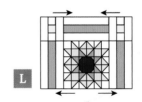

L

5. Join the next block row of 3 blocks and the top sashing row. Sew the side triangles on.

6. Sew sashing rows to both sides of the center block row of 5 blocks. Don't sew the triangles on this row until the end.

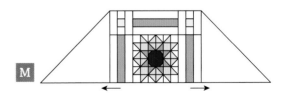

M

7. Sew a sashing row to the bottom of the next row of 3 blocks. Sew the side triangles on.

8. Sew a sashing row to the bottom of the next row of 1 block. Sew the side triangles on.

9. Sew all the rows together. Press toward the sashing.

10. Using the corner triangles cut from the 16½″ square, sew a triangle to each of the corners. Fold the triangles in half to mark the center. Alight the center of the triangle to the center of the block for accuracy. There will be excess fabric at each side.

11. To square up the quilt top, align the ¼″ mark on your ruler with the outer points of the sashing corners. Use a rotary cutter and trim the excess fabric. This allows a ¼″ seam allowance. Square up each side of the quilt.

12. Measure the quilt top through the center of the quilt in both directions. This will give you an accurate length for the borders. The quilt should measure approximately 76½″ square at this point. When working with bias triangles the size of the quilt may vary slightly. Measuring your quilt will give you the best measurement for the borders. Cut the borders as listed under Cutting, making adjustments as needed.

13. Sew the side borders to the quilt front. Press.

14. Sew the top and bottom borders to the quilt front. Press.

Finishing

For more details, see Finishing (page 109).

1. Baste the quilt backing, batting, and quilt top together. Hand or machine quilt as desired. This quilt was machine quilted with a sunflower design.

2. Make the binding and attach it to the quilt.

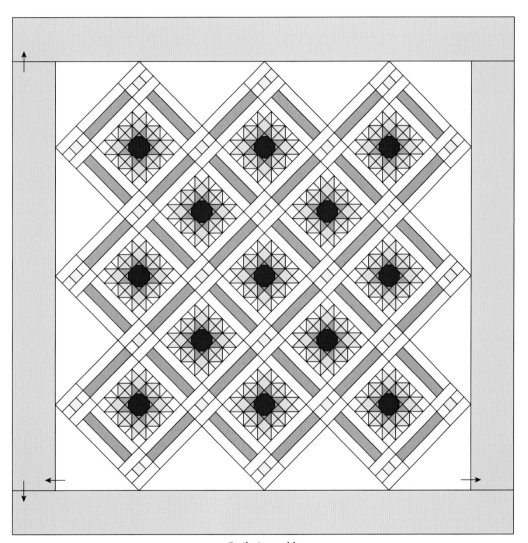

Quilt Assembly

mod diamonds

Mid Century design is my favorite! I love the art, the furniture, the clothing, the cars, and the colors from this era. *Mod Diamonds* is inspired by mid-century style with a touch of whimsy. This quilt uses only one quilt block and the design creates a secondary pattern. You can use solid colors and background for a very minimalist version or use your favorite fabric collection. Using 10″ precut squares and the Stitch and Flip Method (page 108) means this quilt comes together in a snap.

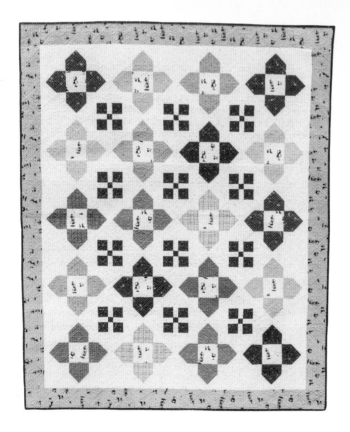

materials

10″ × 10″ PRECUT SQUARES: 1 pack including a minimum of the following:

  20 high volume squares

  5 low volume squares for centers (or yardage for fussy cutting)

RED: 1 fat quarter for cornerstones

CREAM: 3¼ yards for blocks, sashing, and inner border

AQUA: 1⅓ yards for outer border

BINDING: ¾ yard

BACKING: 5 yards

TIP I love quilt blocks that allow for a fussy cut theme print in the center. To fussy cut, use a 4½″ × 4½″ clear template. Center the template over the theme print fabric. Use a rotating cutting mat so you don't have to lift or reposition the template. For larger prints, you will need extra yardage.

Fabrics used in this quilt are Mod Meow by Amanda Niederhauser for Riley Blake Designs.

WOFQ is width of fat quarter

Precut Squares

• From each of the 20 high-volume 10″ squares, cut 4 squares 4½″ × 4½″.

• From each of the 5 low volume 10″ squares, cut 4 squares 4½″ × 4½″. (Or from optional theme print yardage fussy cut 20 squares 4½″ × 4½″.)

Red Fat Quarter

• Cut 6 strips 2½″ × WOFQ, subcut into 48 squares 2½″ × 2½″.

• Cut 1 strip 1½″ × WOFQ, subcut into 12 squares 1½″ × 1½″.

Cream

• Cut 10 strips 2½″ × WOF, subcut into 160 squares 2½″ × 2½″.

• Cut 4 strips 4½″ × WOF, subcut into 31 squares 4½″ × 4½″.

• Cut 3 strips 4½″ × WOF, subcut into 48 rectangles 4½″ × 2½″.

• Cut 3 strips 2½″ × WOF, subcut into 48 squares 2½″ × 2½″.

• Cut 2 strips 12½″ × WOF, subcut into 31 rectangles 12½″ × 1½″.

• Cut 8 strips 1½″ × WOF, piece end to end. Subcut into 2 side inner borders 64½″ × 1½″ and 2 top and bottom inner borders 53½″ × 1½″. (Wait to cut until quilt top is made and measured.)

Aqua

• Cut 8 strips 4½″ × WOF, piece end to end. Subcut into 2 side outer borders 66½″ × 4½″ and 2 top and bottom outer borders 61½″ × 4½″. (Wait to cut until quilt top is made and measured.)

Binding

• Cut 8 strips 2½″ × WOF.

Making the Mod Diamond Block

All seams are ¼″ unless otherwise noted. Follow the pressing arrows shown in the illustrations.

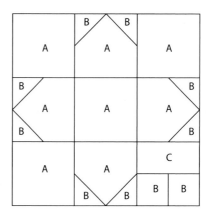

Block Diagram
A: 4½″ × 4½″   •   B: 2½″ × 2½″   •   C: 2½″ × 4½″

1. Referring to the Stitch and Flip Method (page 108), sew a cream 2½″ × 2½″ square to the top right and left corners of a high volume 4½″ × 4½″ square. Trim ¼″ away from the seam and press towards the triangle. Repeat with each of the high volume 4½″ × 4½″ squares.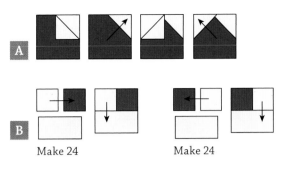

2. Make a corner square by using a cream 2½″ × 2½″ square, a red 2½″ × 2½″ square, and a 2½″ × 4½″ cream rectangle. Sew the squares together and press. Sew the rectangle to the unit and press. Make 24 units with the red square in the right corner and 24 units with the red square in the left corner. **B**

3. Lay out the blocks following the Corner Unit Placement Guide. The position of the block in the quilt will determine how many corner units and where they are positioned. Where there are no corner units, use a 4½″ × 4½″ cream square. **C**

4. Sew the block together as you would a 9 patch by sewing the 3 units together in each row and then sewing the 3 rows together. **D**

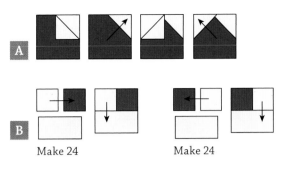

Make 24   Make 24

Corner Unit Placement Guide

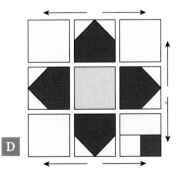

Assembling the Quilt

1. To make a sashing row, sew 3 red cornerstones 1½″ × 1½″ between 4 sashing rectangles 12½″ × 1½″. Repeat to make 4 sashing rows. Press.

2. To make a block row, sew 3 sashing rectangles 12½″ × 1½″ between each of 4 blocks. Press. Make 5 block rows.

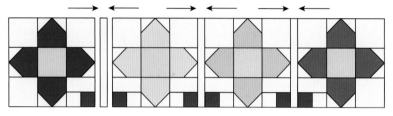

3. Sew the quilt together in rows, alternating the sashing rows and the block rows. Press.

4. Sew the side inner borders to the quilt front. Press.

5. Sew the top and bottom inner borders to the quilt front. Press.

6. Sew the side outer borders to the quilt front. Press.

7. Sew the top and bottom outer borders to the quilt front. Press.

Finishing

For more details, see Finishing (page 109).

1. Baste the quilt backing, batting, and quilt top together. Hand or machine quilt as desired. This quilt was machine quilted with a retro tile design.

2. Make the binding and attach it to the quilt.

Quilt Assembly

playful pinwheels

I love how whimsical pinwheel quilts are. What I don't love is cutting a bunch of triangles. This method uses "squares only" cutting which makes it fast and easy. Use your favorite fat quarters and pair with a natural linen background fabric. I love Riley Blake Designs linen. It's 55% linen and 45% cotton which means it doesn't wrinkle as much as 100% linen. I love how it gives quilts a nice earthy, natural texture.

materials

FAT QUARTERS: 11 including:

  10 print fat quarters

  1 white fat quarter

HUNTER GREEN: 1 yard

NATURAL LINEN: 3 yards for blocks and sashing

FLORAL: 1¼ yards for border

BINDING: ¾ yard

BACKING: 5¼ yards

Fabric is Daisy Fields by Bev McCollough for Riley Blake Designs.

cutting

Fat Quarters

- From each of the 10 print fat quarters, cut 2 strips 7″ × WOFQ (21″), subcut into 4 squares 7″ × 7″. Make sure you have 10 sets of 4 matching 7″ squares.

- From white fat quarter, cut 3 strips 4″ × WOFQ, subcut into 15 squares 4″ × 4″.

Hunter green

- Cut 4 strips 7½″ × WOF, subcut into 20 squares 7½″ × 7½″.

Natural linen

- Cut 4 strips 7½″ × WOF, subcut into 20 squares 7½″ × 7½″.

- Cut 5 strips 12½″ × WOF, subcut into 49 rectangles 3½″ × 12½″ for sashing.

- Cut 2 strips 4″ × WOF, subcut into 15 squares 4″ × 4″ for sashing.

Floral

- Cut 8 strips 4½″ × WOF, sew strips lengthwise together in pairs. Subcut into 2 side borders 78½″ × 4½″ and 2 top and bottom borders 71½″ × 4½″. (Wait to cut until quilt top is made and measured.)

Binding

- Cut 8 strips 2½″ × WOF.

Making the Twirl Block

All seams are ¼″ unless otherwise noted. Follow the pressing arrows shown in the illustrations.

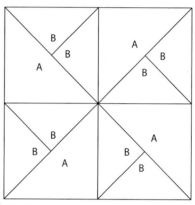

Block Diagram
A: 7″ • B: 7½″

....

TIP Instead of measuring and cutting triangles and worrying about bias edges, the Split Quarter Square Triangles method allows you to use squares to get the split quarter square triangles. However, each set will yield 4 units twirling right and 4 units twirling left. Make sure to gather units that are the same twirling direction to make the block. You can arrange the blocks any way you want in the quilt. The wide sashing provides a lot of separation so you don't notice the twirls going in different directions.

1. Make 40 HSTs using the 7½″ hunter green squares and 7½″ linen squares and referring to Making Two Half-Square Triangles (page 108). Don't worry about squaring up the HSTs just yet.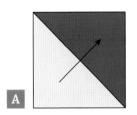

2. Draw a diagonal line on the wrong side of a 7″ print square. Center the print square on top of a HST, right sides together, with the diagonal line perpendicular to the HST seam. The squares will not be the same size—the HST will be slightly larger (it's okay, you will square everything up at the end).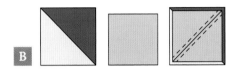

3. Sew ¼″ away from both sides of the diagonal line. Cut on the diagonal line, and press toward the print fabric. Trim the split quarter square triangle to measure 6½″ × 6½″. Repeat with the rest of the 4 matching print squares. You will have 8 split quarter square triangles, which is enough for 2 blocks.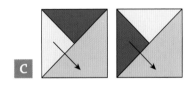

4. Divide your split quarter square triangles into 2 piles for the 2 twirl blocks. It's important to note that 4 pinwheels will be twirling to the right and 4 to the left. Make sure you gather up 4 matching split pinwheel units to make each twirl block.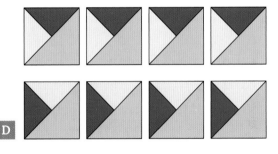

5. Layout the twirl blocks and sew them together as you would a 4-Patch. Press.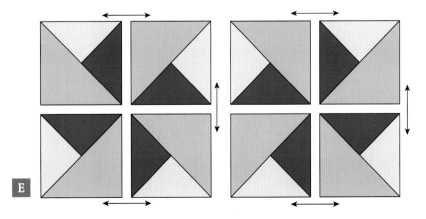

6. Repeat steps 2–5 with each of the print 7″ squares. Make 20 total twirl blocks. Blocks measure 12½″ × 12½″ at this point.

Assembling the Quilt

1. Make 30 HSTs using the 4˝ white squares and 4˝ linen squares and referring to Making Two Half-Square Triangles (page 108). Square up the HSTs to measure 3½˝ × 3½˝.

2. To make a sashing row, sew 5 white/linen HSTs between and at each end of 4 sashing rectangles 12½˝ × 3½˝. Make 6 sashing rows.

3. To make a block row, sew 5 sashing rectangles 12½˝ × 3½˝ between and at each end of 4 blocks. Make 5 block rows.

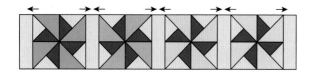

4. Sew the quilt together in rows, alternating the sashing rows and block rows.

5. Sew the side floral borders to the quilt front. Press.

6. Sew the top and bottom floral borders to the quilt front. Press.

Finishing

For more details, see Finishing (page 109).

1. Baste the quilt backing, batting, and quilt top together. Hand or machine quilt as desired. This quilt was machine quilted with a rainbow design.

2. Make the binding and attach it to the quilt.

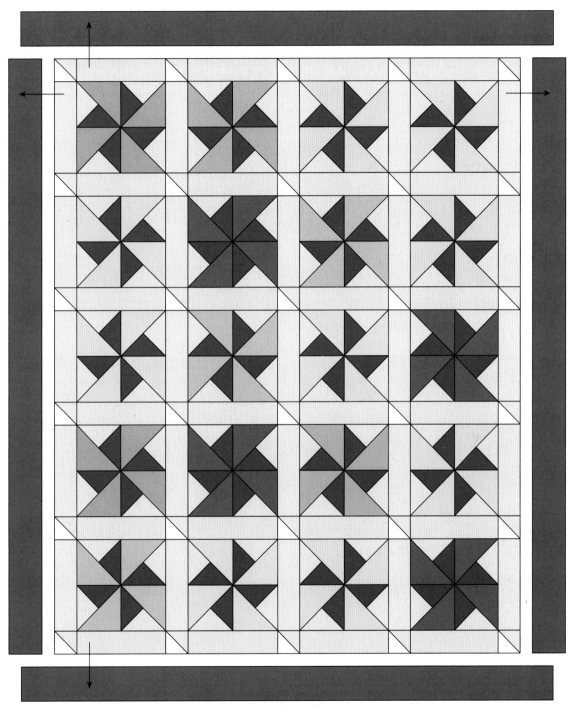

Quilt Assembly

strawberry farm

Living in California means fresh strawberries all year round. I love making strawberry jam, strawberry pie, and strawberry shortcake! This quilt is sure to make your mouth water. Using 5 shades of pink/red gives each strawberry block an ombré look just like real strawberries have.

materials

2½" × WOF PRECUT STRIPS: 1 roll including the following:

   5 light pink strips for strawberries

   5 dark pink strips for strawberries

   5 light red strips for strawberries

   5 medium red strips for strawberries

   5 dark red strips for strawberries

   5 medium green strips for stem and leaves

   4 light green strips for accents

DARK GREEN: ½ yard for Pinwheel block

MEDIUM GREEN: ½ yard for Pinwheel block

DARK GREEN: 1 fat quarter for cornerstones

WHITE: 4¾ yards for blocks and sashing

RED: 1 yard for border

BINDING: ¾ yard

BACKING: 7¼ yards

Fabrics in this quilt are Red Hot by Riley Blake Designs and an assortment of Riley Blake Designs basic greens, pinks, and white.

Precut Strips

- From each of the 5 light pink 2½˝ strips, cut 6 rectangles 4˝ × 2½˝ and 3 rectangles 5½˝ × 2½˝.

- From each of the 5 dark pink, light red, medium red, and dark red 2½˝ strips, cut 3 rectangles 12½˝ × 2½˝.

- From each of the 5 medium green 2½˝ strips cut:

12 squares 2½˝ × 2½˝

3 rectangles 2½˝ × 1½˝

- From the 4 light green 2½˝ strips, cut 60 squares 2½˝ × 2½˝.

Dark Green

- Cut 3 strips 4˝ × WOF, subcut into 30 squares 4˝ × 4˝.

Medium Green

- Cut 6 strips 2˝ × WOF.

White

- For the Strawberry Blocks:

Cut 1 strip 1½˝ × WOF, subcut into 15 squares 1½˝ × 1½˝.

Cut 2 strips 4˝ × WOF, subcut into 30 rectangles 2½˝ × 4˝.

Cut 4 strips 2½˝ × WOF, subcut into 60 squares 2½˝ × 2½˝.

Cut 4 strips 5˝ × WOF, subcut into 30 squares 5˝ × 5˝.

- For the Pinwheel Blocks:

Cut 6 strips 2˝ × WOF.

Cut 6 strips 6½˝ × WOF, subcut into 60 rectangles 6½˝ × 3½˝.

Cut 3 strips 4˝ × WOF, subcut into 30 squares 4˝ × 4˝.

- For the Sashing:

Cut 4 strips 12½˝ × WOF, subcut into 71 rectangles 12½˝ × 2˝.

Red

Cut 8 strips 4˝ × WOF, piece end to end. Press. Subcut into 2 side borders 83˝ × 4˝ and 2 top and bottom borders 75½˝ × 4˝. (Wait to cut until quilt top is made and measured.)

Binding

Cut 9 strips 2½˝ × WOF, piece end to end. Press.

Make the Strawberry Blocks

All seams are ¼˝ unless otherwise noted. Follow the pressing arrows shown in the illustrations.

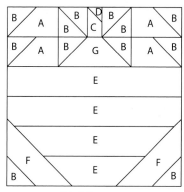

Block Diagram

A: 4˝ × 2½˝   E: 12½˝ × 2½˝
B: 2½˝ × 2½˝   F: 5˝ × 5˝
C: 1½˝ × 2½˝   G: 5½˝ × 2½˝
D: 1½˝ × 1½˝

TIP Arrange each of the 5 strawberry colors in piles so it's easy to assemble each strawberry block. Use lots of different prints for an eclectic look or use solids for a modern look.

1. Gather 2 white rectangles 4″ × 2½″, 2 white squares 2½″ × 2½″, 1 white square 1½″ × 1½″, 2 medium green squares 2½″ × 2½″, and 1 medium green rectangle 1½″ × 2½″.

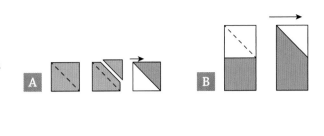

2. Using 2 medium green squares and 2 white squares 2½″ × 2½″, make 2 HSTs using the Making One Half-Square Triangle method (page 108). Press toward the green. **A**

3. Draw a diagonal line on the WS of the white 1½″ square. Position the 1½″ white square RST with the medium green 1½″ × 2½″ rectangle. Sew on the diagonal line. Trim ¼″ away from the seam. Press toward the white. **B**

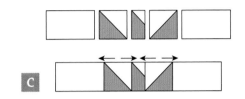

4. Assemble the first row of the Strawberry block. Press. **C**

5. Gather 2 light pink rectangles 4″ × 2½″, 1 light pink rectangle 5½″ × 2½″, and 2 medium green squares 2½″ × 2½″.

6. Draw a diagonal line on the WS of the 2 medium green 2½″ squares. Align a medium green square with the left side of the pink 5½″ rectangle, right sides together. Sew on the diagonal line. Trim ¼″ away from the seam and press. Repeat on the right side. **D**

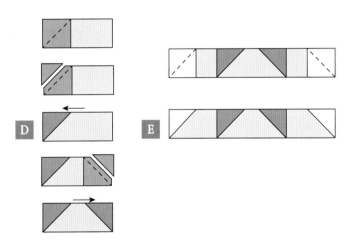

7. Assemble the second row of the Strawberry Block. Draw a diagonal line on the WS of 2 white 2½″ squares. Position them on both ends of the second row unit RST. Sew on the diagonal line. Trim ¼″ away from the seam. Press toward the white. **E**

8. Join the first two rows and the dark pink, light red, medium red, and dark red 12½″ × 2½″ rectangles to make the strawberry block. Press. **F**

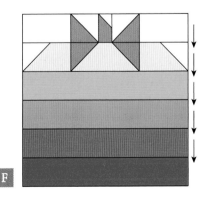

9. Draw a diagonal line on the WS of 2 white squares 5″ × 5″. Position the squares RST on the bottom corners of the Strawberry Block with the diagonal lines making a "V" shape. Sew on the diagonal line. Trim ¼″ away from the seam. Press.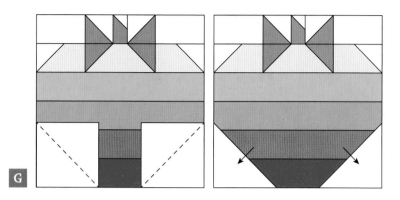

10. Draw a diagonal line on the WS of 4 light green 2½″ squares. Position a light green square in each corner of the strawberry block RST. Sew on the diagonal line and trim ¼″ away from the seam. Press toward the green. The quilt block measures 12½″ × 12½″ at this point. **H**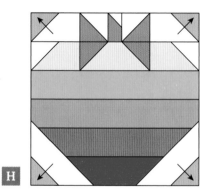

11. Repeat steps 1–10 to make 15 Strawberry Blocks.

Making the Pinwheel Block

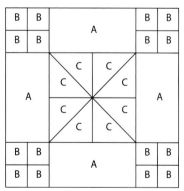

Block Diagram

A: 3½″ × 6½″   C: 4″ × 4″
B: 2″ × 2″

1. Gather the 2″ × WOF medium green and white strips.

2. Sew a medium green 2″ strip to a white 2″ strip lengthwise. Press toward the green. Repeat to make 6 strip sets. Cut each strip set at 2″ increments to make 120 units. **I**

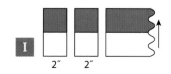

3. Sew 2 pairs together to make a checkerboard unit. Press. Repeat to make 60 checkerboard units.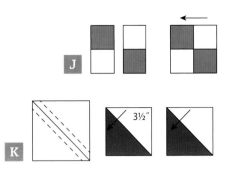

4. Gather the 4″ dark green squares and the 4″ white squares. Draw a diagonal line on the WS of each of the white squares. Pair a white square and a dark green square RST. Refer to Making Two Half-Square Triangles (page 108) and use this method to make a total of 60 half square triangles. Press toward the green. Trim to measure 3½″ × 3½″.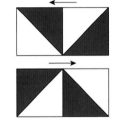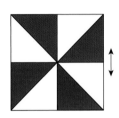

5. Make the center pinwheel unit by using 4 HSTs. Sew them together in a 4-patch. Press. Make 15 pinwheel units.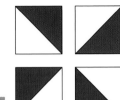

6. Sew a white rectangle 3½″ × 6½″ to both sides of the pinwheel unit. Press. M

7. Sew a checkerboard unit to both ends of 30 white rectangles 3½″ × 6½″. Make sure the green squares form a chain going out from each corner. Press.

8. Sew a checkerboard row to the top and bottom of each pinwheel unit. Press. Make 15 pinwheel blocks. Blocks measure 12½″ × 12½″ at this point. N

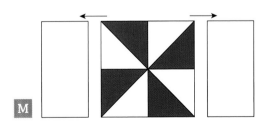

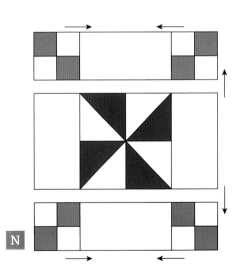

Assembling the Quilt

1. To make a sashing row, sew 6 dark green 2″ cornerstones between and at each end of 5 sashing rectangles 12½″ × 2″. Repeat to make 7 sashing rows.

2. To make a block row, sew 6 sashing rectangles 12½″ × 2″ between and at each end of 5 blocks. Press. Repeat to make 6 block rows.

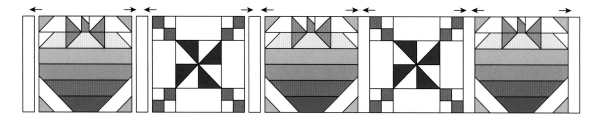

3. Sew the quilt together in rows, alternating the sashing rows and block rows. Press.

4. Sew the side borders to the quilt front. Press.

5. Sew the top and bottom borders to the quilt front. Press.

Finishing

For more details, see Finishing (page 109).

1. Baste the quilt backing, batting, and quilt top together. Hand or machine quilt as desired. This quilt was machine quilted with a feather party design.

2. Make the binding and attach it to the quilt.

Quilt Assembly

FINISHED QUILT: 67" × 82"

summer meadow

I collect star quilts and I am always ready to make another one! This quilt block has a star set in a flower petal design giving it a summer feel. Each of the 20 blocks uses a different fat eighth so you can use a wide variety of fabrics. The sashing forms a frame around each block and this sashing method can be used with any of the quilt blocks in this book.

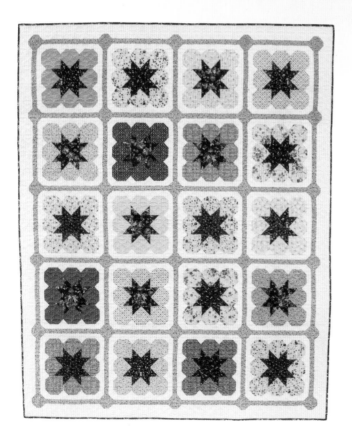

materials

FAT EIGHTHS: 20 of different prints for blocks

FAT QUARTERS: 5 blue fat quarters for center stars

PINK: 1⅛ yards for sashing

WHITE: 3¼ yards for blocks, sashing, and border

BINDING: ¾ yard

BACKING: 5¼ yards

TIP It's easy to customize this quilt! Try Shades of oranges with black centers for Halloween or reds and greens for Christmas.

Fabric is Daisy Fields by Bev McCollough for Riley Blake Designs.

cutting

Fat Eighths

- From each fat eighth, cut 2 strips 4½″ × width of fat eighths, subcut into 8 squares 4½″ × 4½″.

Blue Fat Quarters

- From each blue fat quarter, cut:

  4 strips 2½″ × WOFQ, subcut into 32 squares 2½″ × 2½″

  1 strip 4½″ × WOFQ, subcut into 4 squares 4½″ × 4½″

White

- Cut 16 strips 1½″ × WOF, subcut into 400 squares 1½″ × 1½″.

- Cut 4 strips 12½″ × WOF, subcut into 98 rectangles 1½″ × 12½″ for sashing.

- Cut 5 strips 1½″ × WOF, subcut into 120 squares 1½″ × 1½″.

- Cut 8 strips 2½″ × WOF, sew strips lengthwise together in pairs. Subcut into 2 side borders 2½″ × 78½″ and 2 top and bottom borders 2½″ × 67½″. (Wait to cut until quilt top is made and measured.)

Pink

- Cut 2 strips 12½″ × WOF, subcut into 49 rectangles 1½″ × 12½″.

- Cut 3 strips 3½″ × WOF, subcut into 30 squares 3½″ × 3½″.

Binding

- Cut 9 strips 2½″ × WOF.

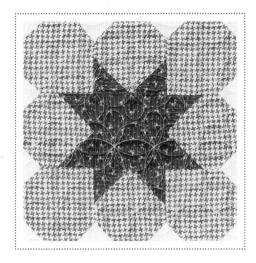

Making the Summer Meadow Block

All seams are ¼″ unless otherwise noted. Follow the pressing arrows shown in the illustrations.

Use the Stitch and Flip method (page 108) for easy triangles.

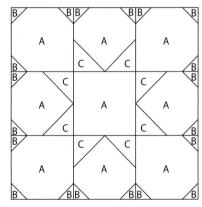

Block Diagram
A: 4½″ × 4½″   C: 2½″ × 2½″
B: 1½″ × 1½″

1. Gather 8 matching 4½″ × 4½″ squares, 20 white squares 1½″ × 1½″, 8 blue 2½″ × 2½″ squares, and 1 blue 4½″ × 4½″ square.

2. Draw a diagonal line on the WS of the white 1½″ squares. Position a 1½″ white square on the top corners of a 4½″ square RST. Sew on the diagonal line. **A**

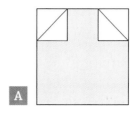

3. Trim ¼″ away from the seam. Press toward the white. Repeat this stitch and flip process making 8 petal units. **B**

4. Using 4 petal units, sew a third white 1½″ square on the bottom left corner. Press. **C**

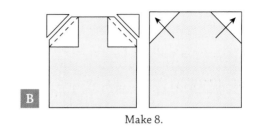

Make 8.

5. Gather the remaining 4 petal units. Draw a diagonal line on the WS of the blue 2½″ squares. Position a blue 2½″ blue square on the bottom left of the petal unit. **D**

6. Sew on the diagonal line and trim ¼″ away from the seam. Press. **E**

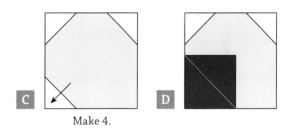

Make 4.

7. Repeat on the right side. Repeat this stitch and flip process to make 4 petal units with star points. **F**

8. Lay out the block as pictured. Sew the block together in rows. Press. Sew the rows together. Press. **G**

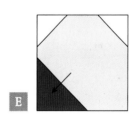

9. Repeat steps 1–8 to make 20 Summer Meadow blocks. Blocks measure 12½″ × 12½″ at this point.

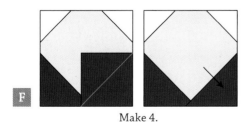

Make 4.

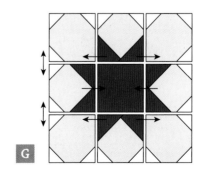

Making the Sashing

TIP Use a little fabric spray starch for small pieces so they don't stretch during pressing. This will help keep the block true to size.

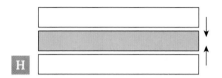

1. Sew a white 1½″ × 12½″ rectangles to either edge of a pink 1½″ × 12½″ rectangle. Press. Repeat to make 49 sashing units. H

2. Draw a diagonal line on the WS of 120 white 1½″ squares. Using the Stitch and Flip method (page 108), position a white square RST each of the 4 corners of a pink 3½″ square. Sew on the diagonal line. Trim ¼″ away from the seam. Press. Repeat to make 30 Snowball blocks. I

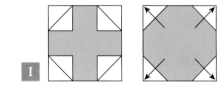

3. To make a sashing row, sew 5 Snowball blocks between and at each end of the rectangle sashing units. Press. Make 6 sashing rows. J

Assembling the Quilt

1. To make the block row, sew a rectangle sashing unit in between and at each end of 4 blocks. Press. Make 5 block rows. K

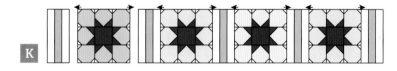

2. Sew the quilt together in rows, alternating the sashing and the block rows. Press the seams as indicated.

3. Sew the side borders to the quilt front. Press.

4. Sew the top and bottom borders to the quilt front. Press.

Finishing

For more details, see Finishing (page 109).

1. Baste the quilt backing, batting, and quilt top together. Hand or machine quilt as desired. This quilt was machine quilted with a Loop T Loop design.

2. Make the binding and attach it to the quilt.

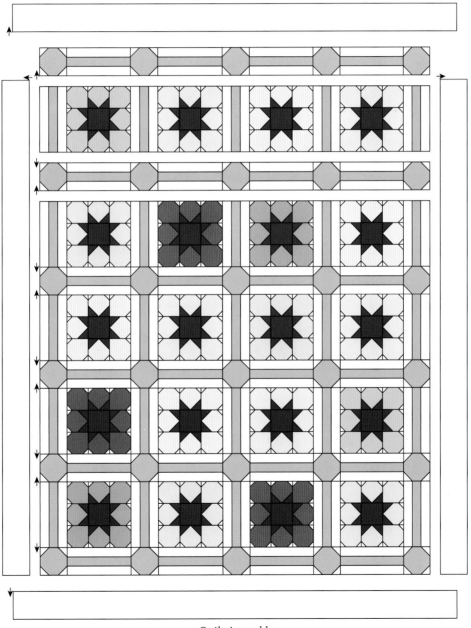

Quilt Assembly

happy scrappy

Setting blocks on point gives a new look to simple blocks. I love quilts that are scrappy. This is the perfect quilt to use up 2½″ strips. You can choose fabrics that are super random including blacks, reds, pastels, and bolds for a really scrappy look. Or choose a color palette to keep it more tranquil. I avoided really dark colors and I kept my fabrics in the pink, yellow, blue, green range.

materials

2½″ × WOF PRECUT STRIPS: 1½ rolls including the following:

 45 high volume strips for Scrappy blocks

 12 high volume strips for Cross block

PALE PINK*: 3 yards for Cross block and setting triangles

BINDING: ¾ yard

BACKING: 5½ yards

*I used a pale pink linen blend for the background of this quilt. It gives it a nice soft feel both in texture and color. Get creative on your background fabric!

TIP The Scrappy block is made up of 36 squares 2½″ × 2½″. You can always cut 36 squares and sew them together individually. To save time I like to use a method where you sew strips together and then cut the strips. This avoids having to cut 720 individual squares.

cutting

Precut 2½″ Strips

- Cut each of the 45 Scrappy block strips in half yielding 2 pieces 2½″ × 21″ for a total of 90 strips.

- Cut each of the 12 Cross block strips into 2 rectangles 4½″ × 2½″ and 2 rectangles 8½″ × 2½″.

Pale pink

- Cut 3 strips 2½″ × WOF, subcut into 48 squares 2½″ × 2½″.

- Cut 6 strips 2½″ × WOF, subcut into 24 rectangles 2½″ × 8½″.

- Cut 1 strip 12½″ × WOF, subcut into 16 rectangles 12½″ × 2½″.

- Cut 3 strips 2½″ × WOF, subcut into 8 rectangles 12½″ × 2½″.

- Cut 2 strips 19″ × WOF, subcut into 4 squares 19″ × 19″. Cut twice diagonally to yield 14 setting triangles.

- Cut 1 strip 10″ × WOF, subcut into 2 squares 10″ × 10″. Cut once diagonally to yield 4 corner triangles.

Binding

- Cut 8 strips 2½″ × WOF.

Making the Scrappy Block

All seams are ¼″ unless otherwise noted. Follow the pressing arrows shown in the illustrations.

TIP Since we are cutting through a lot of seams, shorten the stitch length on your sewing machine. This will help the seams stay together and reduce the likelihood of unraveling.

1. To get a super scrappy look, mix up all the 2½″ × 21″ strips and don't worry about color placement. Gather strips in pairs and sew together. **A**

2. Sew together 3 pairs so you have 6 strips sewn together. Press in one direction. Repeat to make 15 strip units. **B**

3. Subcut the strip units in 2½″ increments. You will get 8 scrappy units per strip unit. After cutting all the strip units you will have 120 scrappy units 12½″ × 2½″. **C**

4. Mix up all the scrappy units. Sew 6 scrappy units together to form a block measuring 12½″ × 12½″. Repeat to make 20 blocks. **D**

Making the Cross Block

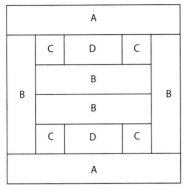

Block Diagram

A: 12½″ × 2½″   C: 2½″ × 2½″
B: 8½″ × 2½″   D: 4½″ × 2½″

1. Gather the print rectangles 2½″ × 4½″ and 8½″ × 2½″ and the background 2½″ squares and rectangles 8½″ × 2½″ and 12½″ × 2½″.

2. Sew 2 matching print 8½″ rectangles together. Press. **E**

3. Sew a white 2½″ square to both sides of a matching 4½″ × 2½″ rectangle. Press. Make 2. **F**

4. Sew each to the top and bottom of the center unit. Press. **G**

5. Sew a white rectangle 2½″ × 8½″ to both sides of the center unit. Press. **H**

6. Sew a white rectangle 2½″ × 12½″ to the top and bottom of the unit. Press. Repeat to make 12 Cross blocks. The block measures 12½″ × 12½″ at this point. **I**

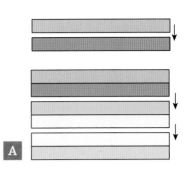

A

B

Make 15 strip units.

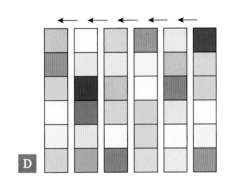

C

2½″ 2½″ 2½″

Cut at 2½″ increments.

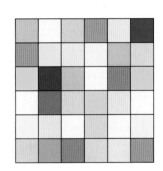

D

E

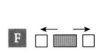

F

G

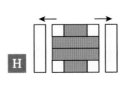

H

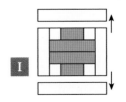

I

Assembling the Quilt

1. Lay out the quilt blocks and triangles according to the quilt diagram (page 51). The quilt blocks are set on point and are sewn in diagonal rows. The Scrappy block and Cross blocks are alternated.

Begin in the upper left corner. The first row has one Scrappy block. It begins and ends with a setting triangle. The next row has 3 blocks (2 Scrappy and 1 Cross) and begins and ends with a setting triangle, and so on.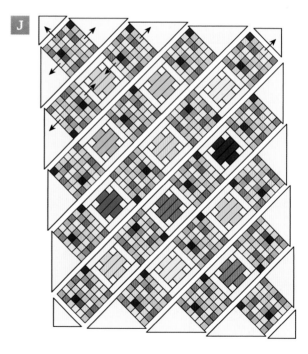

2. Sew the rows together and press all the seams in one direction.

> **TIP** It can get a bit bulky to keep adding one row to the quilt. I assemble my quilt in 2 sections or halves, then sew the sections together. This makes it a little easier to work with.

3. Add the corner triangles after the rows are sewn together.

4. To straighten the quilt top, align a ruler with the outermost points of the blocks. Use the ¼″ mark and align with each of the points. Use a rotary cutter to trim the excess fabric. This leaves a ¼″ seam allowance.

Finishing

For more details, see Finishing (page 109).

1. Baste the quilt backing, batting, and quilt top together. Hand or machine quilt as desired. This quilt was machine quilted with a rippled flower design.

2. Make the binding and attach it to the quilt.

> **TIP** Since this quilt is so scrappy I wanted a scrappy binding. I used a variety of 2½″ × WOF strips and cut them at random lengths. Then I sewed them together end to end just like making regular binding. The total binding length required is about 330″.

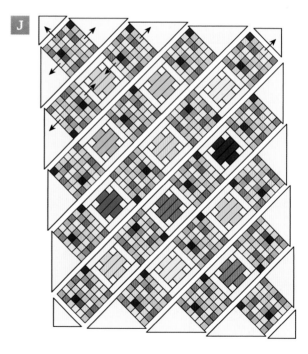

Quilt Assembly

flower crossing

I love quilts that make a secondary design. This quilt uses only one block with some pieced sashing to make it look much more complicated than it really is. Using mostly high-volume precut 10″ squares allows this quilt to have a wide variety of fabric prints. Of course I chose florals!

materials

10″ × 10″ PRECUT SQUARES: 2 packs including the following:

40 high-volume squares

5 low-volume squares

DARK BLUE: 1¼ yards for sashing and inner borders

WHITE: 1¼ yards for blocks

BLUE FLORAL: 1¼ yards for outer borders

BINDING: ¾ yard

BACKING: 5¼ yards

TIP When selecting a prepackaged bundle of 10″ squares, check to see how many low- and high-volume fabrics there are. Not every collection is the same. This quilt requires 40 high-volume 10″ squares, which means you most likely will need 2 bundles.

*Fabrics are Hidden Cottage
by Minki Kim for Riley Blake Designs*

cutting

Begin by dividing the 40 high-volume squares into 2 equal piles. The first pile will be for the outer block pieces and the second pile will be for the inner block pieces.

Pile #1

• From each 10˝ square cut:

4 rectangles 2½˝ × 4½˝

4 squares 2½˝ × 2½˝

Pile #2

• From each 10˝ square cut:

2 rectangles 8½˝ × 2½˝

2 rectangles 2½˝ × 4½˝

Low-volume 10˝ squares

• From each square cut 4 squares 4½˝ × 4½˝.

Dark blue

• Cut 4 strips 4½˝ × WOF.

• Cut 8 strips 2½˝ × WOF, sew lengthwise together in pairs. Subcut into 2 side borders 68½˝ × 2½˝ and 2 top and bottom borders 58½˝ × 2½˝. (Wait to cut until quilt top is made and measured.)

White

• Cut 5 strips 4½˝ × WOF, subcut into 80 rectangles 2½˝ × 4½˝.

• Cut 2 strips 4½˝ × WOF.

• Cut 1 strip 2½˝ × WOF, subcut into 12 squares 2½˝ × 2½˝.

Blue floral

• Cut 8 strips 4½˝ × WOF, sew lengthwise together in pairs. Subcut into 2 side borders 72½˝ × 4½˝ and 2 top and bottom borders 66½˝ × 4½˝. (Wait to cut until quilt top is made and measured.)

Binding

• Cut 8 Strips 2½˝ × WOF.

Making the Flower Crossing Block

A	A	A
B	C	B
A A	D	A A
B	C	B
A	A	A

Block Diagram

A: 4½˝ × 2½˝   C: 8½˝ × 2½˝
B: 2½˝ × 2½˝   D: 4½˝ × 4½˝

1. For each block gather:

From Pile #1, 4 matching rectangles 2½˝ × 4½˝ and their 4 matching squares 2½˝ × 2½˝

From Pile #2, 2 matching rectangles 8½˝ × 2½˝ and their 2 matching rectangles 4½˝ × 2½˝

4 white rectangles 4½˝ × 2½˝

1 low-volume center square 4½˝ × 4½˝

2. Sew the Pile #2 4½″ × 2½″ rectangles to both sides of the center square. Press.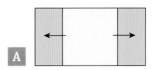

3. Sew the matching 8½″ × 2½″ rectangles to the top and bottom of the center square. Press. **B**

4. Sew the side unit by sewing the Pile #1 2½″ squares to both ends of a white 4½″ × 2½″ rectangle. Press. Make one for each side. **C**

5. Sew the side units to the side of the center block. Press. **D**

6. Sew the top row of the block by sewing the Pile #1 2½″ × 4½″ rectangles to either end of a white rectangle 4½″ × 2½. Press. Repeat to make the bottom row of the block. Press. **E**

7. Sew the top and bottom units to the block. Press. **F**

8. Repeat steps 1–7 to make 20 blocks.

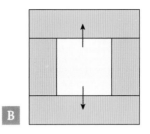

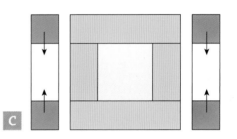

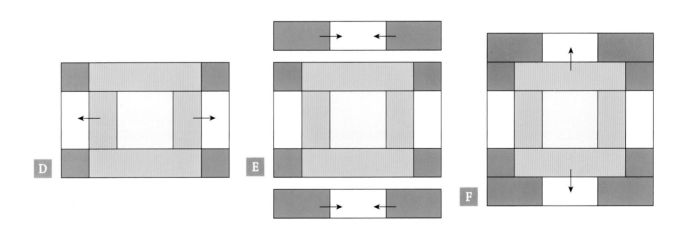

Assembling the Quilt

1. Make the sashing units by sewing a dark blue 4½˝ × WOF strip to both sides of a white 4½˝ × WOF strip lengthwise. Press toward the dark. Repeat to make 2 strip sets. Subcut both strip sets into 2½˝ increments. Make a total of 31 sashing units.

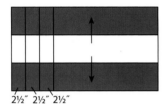

2½˝ 2½˝ 2½˝

2. To make a block row, sew a sashing unit in between each block. Press. Repeat to make 5 block rows.

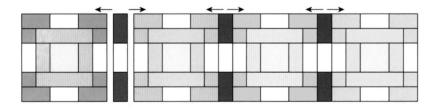

3. To make a sashing row, sew 4 sashing units and 3 white 2½˝ squares together alternately. Press. Repeat to make 4 sashing rows.

4. Sew the rows together. Press.

5. Sew the side inner borders to the quilt front. Press.

6. Sew the top and bottom inner borders to the quilt front. Press.

7. Sew the side outer borders to the quilt front. Press.

8. Sew the top and bottom outer borders to the quilt front. Press.

Finishing

For more details, see Finishing (page 109).

1. Baste the quilt backing, batting, and quilt top together. Hand or machine quilt as desired. This quilt was machine quilted with a compass design.

2. Make the binding and attach it to the quilt.

Quilt Assembly

sweater weather

When September rolls around you can just tell fall is on its way! The air feels crisper and the sky is bluer. Kids are in school, Halloween candy is in the stores, and pumpkins are on the porches. I love everything about fall! This quilt uses all the cozy colors of fall—it makes you want to put on your favorite sweater and walk through the leaves!

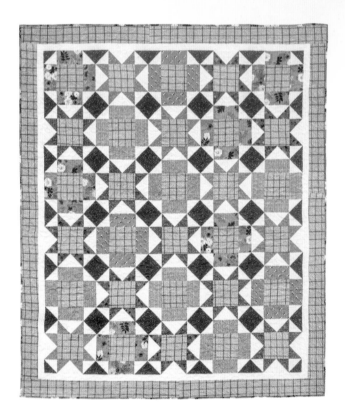

materials

FAT QUARTERS:

5 gold

3 olive green

3 dark mauve

PLAID: 2¼ yards for blocks and outer border

CREAM: 2 yards for blocks and inner border

BINDING: ¾ yard

BACKING: 5¼ yards

*Fabric is Maple, Plaid, and Basics
by Riley Blake Designs.*

cutting

Fat quarters

- From each of 5 gold fat quarters, cut 2 strips 6½″ × WOFQ, subcut into 12 rectangles 6½″ × 3½″ for a total of 60 rectangles.

- From each of 3 olive green fat quarters, cut 4 strips 4″ × WOFQ, subcut into 20 squares 4″ × 4″ for a total of 60 squares.

- From each of 3 dark mauve fat quarters, cut 4 strips 4″ × WOFQ, subcut into 20 squares 4″ × 4″ for a total of 60 squares.

Plaid

- Cut 5 strips 6½″ × WOF, subcut into 30 squares 6½″ × 6½″.

- Cut 8 strips 4½″ × WOF, sew together end-to-end in pairs. Subcut 2 side outer borders 75½″ × 4½″ and 2 top and bottom outer borders 71½″ × 4½″.

Cream

- Cut 3 strips 7¼″ × WOF, subcut into 15 squares 7¼″ × 7¼″.

- Cut 6 strips 4″ × WOF, subcut into 60 squares 4″ × 4″.

- Cut 8 strips 2″ × WOF strips, sew lengthwise together in pairs. Subcut into 2 side inner borders 72½″ × 2″ and 2 top and bottom inner borders 63½″ × 2″. (Wait to cut until quilt top is made and measured.)

Binding

- Cut 8 strips 2½″ × WOF.

> **TIP** It's always easier to press quilt blocks to the dark, however, for this quilt all the block seams will be pressed open. This will allow for all the seam intersections to lay flat.

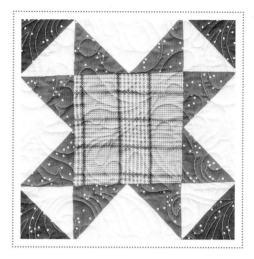

Make the Half Square Triangles

All seams are ¼″ unless otherwise noted. Follow the pressing arrows shown in the illustrations.

1. Gather all the 4″ green squares and all the 4″ cream squares.

2. Draw a diagonal line on the wrong side of all the 4″ cream squares.

3. Pair a green square with a cream square RST. Sew ¼″ away from both sides of the diagonal line. Cut on the diagonal line, yielding 2 HSTs. Press open.

4. Trim to measure 3½″ × 3½″.

5. Repeat making 120 HSTs that will be used in both blocks.

Making the Star Block

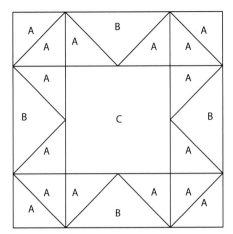

Block Diagram
A: 4″ × 4″ • B: 7¼″ × 7¼″ • C: 6½″ × 6½″

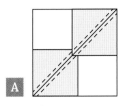

1. Draw a diagonal line on the wrong side of matching 4″ mauve squares.

2. Align 2 marked mauve squares to opposite corners of a 7¼″ cream square, RST. The 2 drawn lines merge into 1 continuous line from corner to corner Sew a scant ¼″ seam on both sides of the continuous line. 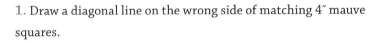 **A**

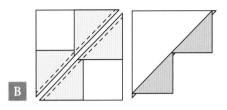

3. Cut on the drawn line to make 2 dog-ear units. Press. **B**

4. Align 1 mauve square to the cream corner of a dog-ear unit. Note that the marked line sits between the dog-ears. Sew a scant ¼″ seam on each side of the drawn line. Cut apart on the line to make 2 flying Geese units. Press toward the star points. Repeat with the second dog-ear unit for a total of 4 Flying Geese units. **C**

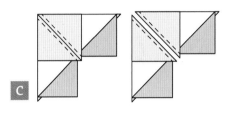

5. Square up each Flying Geese unit to 6½″ × 3½″. **D**

6. Repeat steps 1–4 to make 15 sets of 4 matching Flying Geese units.

7. Lay out the star block using 4 HSTs, 1 set of 4 Flying Geese, and 1 plaid 6½″ square. **E**

8. Sew the block rows together. Press.

9. Sew the rows together. Press.

10. Repeat steps 6–8 to make 15 Star blocks.

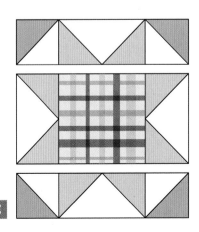

Making the Cross Block

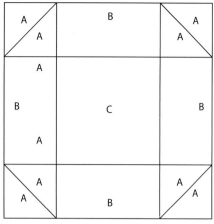

Block Diagram

A: 4″ × 4″ • B: 3½″ × 6½″ • C: 6½″ × 6½″

1. Lay out the block by using 4 HSTs, 4 gold rectangles 3½″ × 6½″, and 1 plaid 6½″ square. **F**

2. Sew the block rows together. Press.

3. Sew the rows together. Press.

4. Repeat to make 15 Cross blocks.

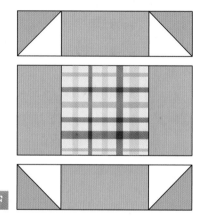

F

> **TIP** I love sashing quilt blocks together but It's also fun to sew quilt blocks directly together. In this quilt alternating the star block and the cross block makes a great secondary pattern.

Assembling the Quilt

1. Lay out the quilt in 6 rows of 5 blocks each. Alternate the star block and the cross block as pictured.

2. Sew the blocks together in rows. Press open.

3. Sew the rows together. Press open.

> **TIP** There are quite a few seam intersections when sewing the blocks and rows together. I like to pin at each seam intersection making sure that the seams match. I use fine pins and sew slowly over them.

4. Sew the inner side borders to the quilt front. Press toward the border.

5. Sew the top and bottom inner borders to the quilt front. Press toward the inner borders.

6. Sew the side outer borders to the quilt front. Press toward the outer borders. Sew the top and bottom outer borders to the quilt front. Press toward the outer border.

Finishing

For more details, see Finishing (page 109).

1. Baste the quilt backing, batting, and quilt top together. Hand or machine quilt as desired. This quilt was machine quilted with a feather swirl design.

2. Make the binding and attach it to the quilt.

Quilt Assembly

woodland christmas

Christmas decorating at my house is all about Christmas trees! I have different themed Christmas trees in each room—and I'm always looking for an excuse to buy another one! It's a fun way to show off what you love. Some of my Christmas tree themes are woodland animals, pink vintage, cats, farmhouse, and family memories. There's just something about Christmas trees! This quilt has 13 tree blocks alternated with a cross block. The sashing creates a secondary pattern which gives the blocks a "bow" look in the corners. You can use your favorite greens for a traditional look or make a bright version with all different colored trees!

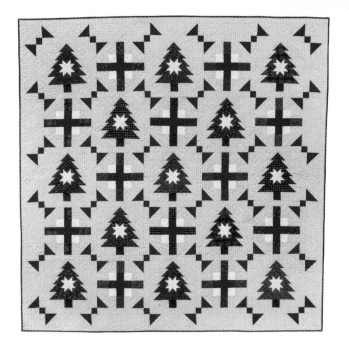

materials

2½˝ × WOF PRECUT STRIPS: 1 bundle including the following:

> 26 strips assorted greens for trees (13 matching pairs)
>
> 7 white strips for stars
>
> 4 dark red strips

BROWN: 1 fat eighth

MEDIUM RED: ¾ yard

LIGHT GRAY LINEN BLEND (OR SIMILAR): 5¼ yards for blocks, sashing, and borders

BINDING: ¾ yard

BACKING: 7¼ yards

Fabric is a variety of fabrics including basics from Riley Blake Designs, background gray linen blend Riley Blake Designs.

cutting

Precut Strips

- Each of the 13 Tree blocks require 2 matching 2½″ × WOF strips—13 pairs for a total of 26 strips. From each pair of strips, cut:

  1 rectangle 4½″ × 2½″

  1 rectangle 6½″ × 2½″

  2 squares 2½″ × 2½″

  2 rectangles 3½″ × 2½″

  1 rectangle 10½″ × 2½″

  4 squares 1½″ × 1½″

  4 squares 2″ × 2″

  From what is remaining of each of the green strips, cut 4 matching rectangles 3½″ × 2½″ for Cross blocks for a total of 12 sets of 4 matching rectangles

- From 1 white strip cut 13 squares 2½″ × 2½″ for star centers.

- From 3 white strips, cut into 3 strips 2″ × WOF, subcut 52 squares 2″ × 2″ for star points.

- Cross Block:

  From 3 white strips, cut 48 squares 2½″ × 2½″.

  From 2 dark red strips 2½″, cut 12 rectangles 6½″ × 2½″.

  From 2 dark red strips 2½″, cut 24 squares 2½″ × 2½″.

Brown

- Cut 13 square 2½″ × 2½″ squares.

Medium Red

- Cut 3 strips 4″ × WOF, subcut into 24 squares 4″ × 4″ for Cross block.

- Cut 2 strips 2″ × WOF, subcut into 36 squares 2″ × 2″ for sashing corners.

- Cut 2 strips 4″ × WOF, subcut into 12 squares 4″ × 4″ for pieced border.

Gray

- Tree Block:

  Cut 2 strips 6½″ × WOF, subcut into 26 rectangles 6½″ × 2½″.

  Cut 2 strips 5½″ × WOF, subcut into 26 rectangles 5½″ × 2½″.

  Cut 2 strips 4½″ × WOF, subcut into 26 rectangles 4½″ × 2½″.

  Cut 4 strips 3½″ × WOF, subcut into 52 rectangles 3½″ × 2½″.

  Cut 2 strips 5½″ × WOF, subcut into 26 rectangles 5½″ × 2½″.

- Cross Block:

  Cut 3 strips 4″ × WOF, subcut into 24 squares 4″ × 4″.

  Cut 6 strips 3½″ × WOF, subcut into 96 rectangles 3½″ × 2½″.

Sashing and borders:

Cut 3 strips 12½″ × WOF, subcut 60 rectangles 12½″ × 2″ sashing rectangles.

Cut 1 strip 6½″ × WOF, subcut into 12 rectangles 6½″ × 3½″ for inner border.

Cut 1 strip 15½″ × WOF, subcut into 8 rectangles 15½″ × 3½″ for inner border.

Cut 1 strip 3½″ × WOF, subcut into 4 rectangles 5″ × 3½″ and 4 rectangles 2″ × 3½″ for inner border.

Cut 2 strips 4″ × WOF, subcut into 12 squares 4″ × 4″ for half square triangles.

Cut 8 strips 2″ × WOF, piece end to end for outer border, subcut into 2 side borders 75½″ × 2″ and 2 top and bottom borders 78½″ × 2″. (Wait to cut until quilt top is made and measured.)

Binding

- Cut 9 strips 2½″ × WOF.

Making the Center Star Block

All seams are ¼″ unless otherwise noted. Follow the pressing arrows shown in the illustrations.

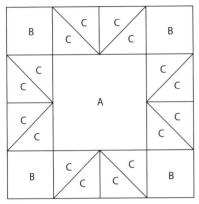

Block Diagram
A: 2½″ × 2½″ · B: 1½″ × 1½″ · C: 2″ × 2″

1. Gather the 13 white squares 2½″ × 2½″, the 52 white squares 2″ × 2″, all the green squares 1½″ × 1½″ and green squares 2″ × 2″.

2. Using the 2″ green squares and 2″ white squares, refer to Making 2 Half- Square Triangles (page 108) to make the HSts. Make a total of 104 green/white HSTs. Trim to measure 1½″ × 1½″.

3. Lay out the star block using 8 green/white HSTs, 4 green squares 1½″ × 1½″, and 1 white square 2½″ × 2½″.

4. Sew the HST units together. Press open.

5. Sew the block together in rows. Press.

6. Sew the rows together. Press.

7. The Star block measures 4½″ × 4½″ at this point.

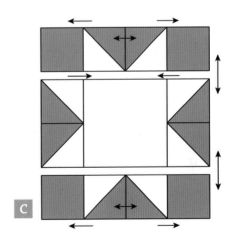

8. Repeat to make 13 Star blocks.

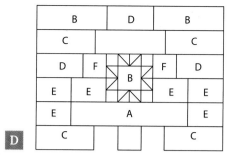

A: 10½″ × 2½″ • B: 6½″ × 2½″ • C: 5½″ × 2½″
D: 4½″ × 2½″ • E: 3½″ × 2½″ • F: 2½″ × 2½″

Making the Tree Block

1. Layout the tree block according to the diagram. Place a Star block in the center of the tree layout.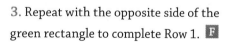

2. Begin with the top 6½″ × 2½″ gray rectangles and 4½″ × 2½″ green rectangle. Put them right sides together at a 90° angle. Use a marking pencil to mark the diagonal line on the WS of the gray rectangle. Sew along the drawn line. Trim ¼″ from the seam. Press toward the gray (refer to The Stitch and Flip Method, page 108). **E**

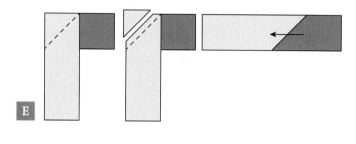

3. Repeat with the opposite side of the green rectangle to complete Row 1. **F**

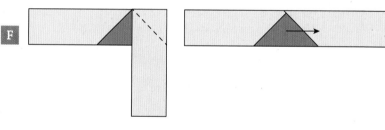

4. For Row 2, sew a 5½″ × 2½″ gray rectangle to the left side of the 6½″ × 2½″ green rectangle perpendicularly, just as you did in step 2. **G**

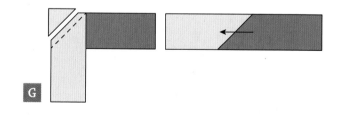

5. Repeat on the opposite end of the green rectangle. **H**

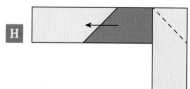

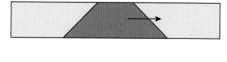

6. For the left end of row 3, sew a gray 4½″ × 2½″ rectangle to a 2½″ × 2½″ green square perpendicularly. Make sure to sew the correct angle.

7. Repeat step 6 to make the opposite end of row 3. Make sure to sew the correct angle. **I**

8. For the left end of Row 4, sew a gray 3½″ × 2½″ rectangle to a 3½″ × 2½″ green square perpendicularly. Make sure to sew the correct angle.

9. Repeat step 8 to make the opposite end of row 4. Make sure to sew the correct angle. **J**

10. Sew the row 3 and row 4 units together. **K**

11. Sew the units to the center star block, making the tree center unit. **L**

12. For Row 5, sew a 3½″ × 2½″ gray rectangle to the left end of the 10½″ × 2½″ green rectangle perpendicularly. Repeat on the opposite end of the green rectangle. **M**

13. For Row 6, sew a 5½″ × 2½″ gray rectangle to both sides of a brown 2½″ × 2½″ square.

14. Sew Rows 1 and 2 together, then sew to the center tree unit.

15. Sew Rows 5 and 6 together, then sew to the center tree unit. **N**

16. Repeat to make 13 Tree blocks. Blocks measure 12½″ × 12½″ at this point.

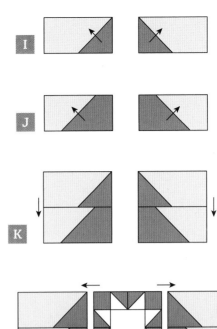

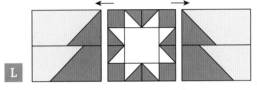

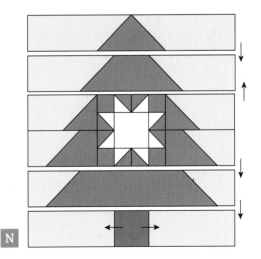

Making the Cross Block

D D	C	C	C	D D
C	B	B	B	C
C		A		C
C	B	B	B	C
D D	C	C	C	D D

Block Diagram

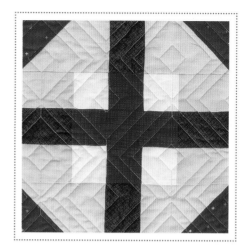

A: 2½″ × 6½″   C: 2½″ × 3½″
B: 2½″ × 2½″   D: 4″ × 4″ = 3½″ × 3½″ HST

1. Refer to Making Two Half-Square Triangles (page 108). Using the red 4″ squares and the gray 4″ squares, make 48 HSTs for the blocks and 24 HSTs for the pieced border. Square up to measure 3½″ × 3½″. Set aside the 24 HSTs for the border. O

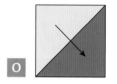

2. Gather the gray and green rectangles 2½″ × 3½″, 48 HSTs, the white and red 2½″ squares, and the red 2½″ × 6½″ rectangles. Layout the block.

3. Sew the block together in rows. Press according to the arrows so seams nest.

4. Sew the rows together. Blocks measure 12½″ × 12½″ at this point. P

5. Repeat steps 2–4 to make 12 Cross blocks.

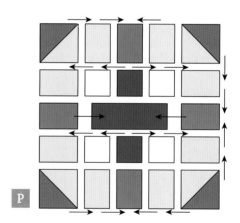

Assembling the Quilt

1. To make a sashing row, sew 6 red sashing cornerstones 2″ × 2″ between and at each end of 5 gray rectangles 12½″ × 2″. Press. Make 6 sashing rows.

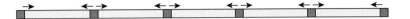

2. To make a block row, sew a gray sashing rectangle 12½″ × 2″ between and at each end of 5 blocks. Press. Make 5 block rows.

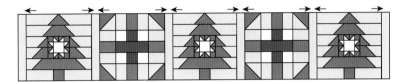

3. Sew the quilt together in rows, alternating the sashing rows and block rows.

4. To make the pieced border, gather the gray:

   2″ × 3½″ rectangles

   5″ × 3½″ rectangles

   6½″ × 3½″ rectangles

   15½″ × 3½″ rectangles

Set aside the 24 gray/red HSTs.

5. Sew together 2 rectangles 2″ × 3½″, 3 rectangles 6½″ × 3½″, 2 rectangles 15½″ × 3½″, and 6 gray/red HSTs to make a side border. Repeat to make 2 side borders.

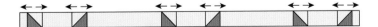

6. Sew together 2 rectangles 5″ × 3½″, 3 rectangles 6½″ × 3½″, 2 rectangles 15½″ × 3½″, and 6 gray/red HSTs to make the top border. Repeat to make the bottom borders.

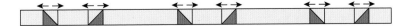

7. Sew the side pieced borders to the quilt front.

8. Sew the top and bottom pieced borders to the front of the quilt.

9. Sew the side outer borders to the quilt front.

10. Sew the top and bottom outer borders to the quilt front.

> **TIP** Whenever an edge of a quilt design has points such as half square triangles or flying geese, I like to add a narrow additional border to ensure the points don't get lost in the binding. Binding tends to puff slightly around the quilt so points that you worked so hard on can get lost. This quilt has a finished 1½″ outer border to allow space in between the pieced border and the binding.

Finishing

For more details, see Finishing (page 109).

1. Baste the quilt backing, batting, and quilt top together. Hand or machine quilt as desired. This quilt was machine quilted with a Squared Off design.

2. Make the binding and attach it to the quilt.

Quilt Assembly

liberty stars

Relaxed and casual quilts are great for picnics, ball games, and beach trips. Nothing says relaxed like chambray! Chambray is a light and airy fabric made of a dyed yarn and a white yarn woven together. This quilt uses large chambray squares alternated between star blocks. It's a fast way to sew a quilt together and a fun way to show off quilting designs. Chambray matches most color schemes and is easy to work with.

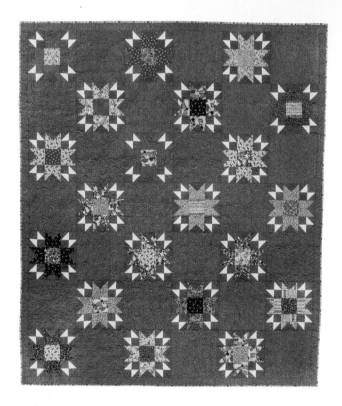

materials

2½˝ × WOF PRECUT STRIPS: 1 pack including a minimum of the following:

  21 strips for star points

  10 strips assorted prints for scrappy binding

5˝ × 5˝ Precut Squares: 21 squares for star centers

CHAMBRAY: 5¾ yards for blocks, squares, and borders

WHITE: ¾ yard

BACKING: 7¼ yards

TIP Since the center squares are different from the star points, consider using your favorite theme prints or large patterns. In this quilt I mixed up the fabrics so the centers coordinate with the points.

Fabric is Carnaby Collection by Liberty Fabrics and chambray by Riley Blake Designs.

cutting

Precut Strips

- From each of the 21 precut star point strips, cut 4 rectangles 4½″ × 2½″, and 8 squares 2½″ × 2½″. Keep the rectangles and squares cut from the same strip together in sets. They will be used in the same block.

Precut Squares

- From each precut square, cut 1 square 4½″ × 4½″.

Chambray

- Cut 7 strips 3″ × WOF, subcut into 84 squares 3″ × 3″.

- Cut 11 strips 2½″ × WOF, subcut into 168 squares 2½″ × 2½″.

- Cut 6 strips 4½″ × WOF, subcut into 84 rectangles 4½″ × 2½″.

- Cut 7 strips 12½″ × WOF, subcut 21 squares 12½″ × 12½″.

- Cut 9 strips 2½″ × WOF, piece end to end and subcut into 2 side borders 84½″ × 2½″ and top and bottom borders 76½″ × 2½″. (Wait to cut until quilt top is made and measured.)

White

- Cut 7 strips 3″ × WOF, subcut into 84 squares 3″ × 3″.

Binding

- Using the 10 precut binding strips, cut at a few random increments and sew together end-to-end to form one continuous scrappy binding strip about 350″ long.

Making the Star Block

Block Diagram

A: 2½″ × 2½″   C: 4½″ × 2½″
B: 3″ × 3″   D: 4½″ × 4½″

Corner Units

1. Gather the 84 chambray and 84 white squares 3″ × 3″.

2. Draw a diagonal line on the back of each white square. Pair a white square with a chambray square right sides together.

3. Refer to Making Two Half-Square Triangles (page 108) and make 168 HSTs.

4. Square up the HSTs to measure 2½″ × 2½″.

5. Gather the 168 chambray 2½″ squares and the HSTs. Make the corner four-patch units. Press. Make 84 corner units.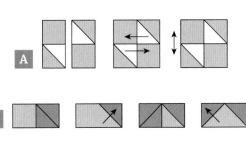

Flying Geese Units

1. Gather 4 chambray rectangles 2½″ × 4½″ and 8 matching print 2½″ squares.

2. Draw a diagonal line on the wrong side of the 8 squares. Position a square on a chambray rectangle, RST at one end. Sew along the diagonal line.

3. Trim ¼″ away from the diagonal line. Press.

4. Repeat on the opposite end of the rectangle.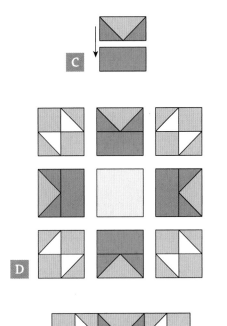

5. Sew a matching rectangle to the bottom of each Flying Geese unit. Press.

6. Repeat to make 84 Flying Geese Units.

Assembling the Block

1. Lay out the block as a nine-patch with the corner units in the corner, the geese units on the sides, and 4½″ square in the center.

2. Sew the units together in rows.

3. Sew the rows together to complete the block. Blocks measure 12½″ at this point.

4. Repeat to make 21 blocks.

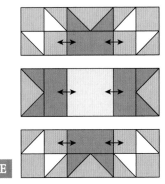

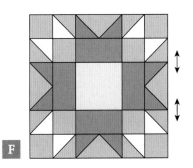

Assembling the Quilt

1. Refer to the quilt assembly diagram and lay out the quilt alternating star blocks and chambray squares.

2. Sew the blocks and squares together. Press.

3. Sew the rows together. Press.

4. Sew the side borders to the quilt front. Press.

5. Sew the top and bottom borders to the quilt front. Press.

Finishing

For more details, see Finishing (page 109).

1. Baste the quilt backing, batting, and quilt top together. Hand or machine quilt as desired. This quilt was machine quilted with a paisley design.

2. Make the binding and attach it to the quilt.

TIP For a fast and easy quilt, use any quilt block in this book and simply alternate with a square of your favorite background fabric. This makes a quilt come together quickly and a fun way to show off the blocks.

Quilt Assembly

modern farmhouse

There is something comforting and calming about the neutral palette of farmhouse décor. This farmhouse-inspired quilt uses neutral tones of gray, greige, and brown against a cream background. The quilt is made of 2 blocks that are alternated, creating a chain effect. No sashing required! Hang this quilt on your wall, lay it over a couch, or roll it up in a basket; it's sure to bring a cozy feel to your farmhouse décor.

materials

FAT EIGHTHS: 15 gray/greige/brown

CREAM: 3¾ yards for blocks and border

DARK GRAY: ⅔ yard

BEIGE: 1¼ yards for outer border

BINDING: ¾ yard

BACKING: 5¼ yards

Fabrics are a variety of fabrics from Riley Blake Designs, background Bee Cross Stitch by Riley Blake Designs.

cutting

Fat Eighths

- Turn the fat eighth sideways so you are cutting off the length. From each fat eighth, cut:

  1 strip 6½″ and subcut into 1 square 6½″ × 6½″ for star center

  4 squares 4″ × 4″ for star points from the remaining piece (14½″ × 9″)

Cream

- Cut 3 strips 7¼″ × WOF, subcut into 15 squares 7¼″ × 7¼″ for Star block.

- Cut 3 strips 3½″ × WOF, subcut into 60 rectangles 3½″ × 2″ for Star block.

- Cut 3 strips 2″ × WOF, subcut into 60 squares 2″ × 2″ for Star block.

- Cut 5 strips 2½″ × WOF, for Cross block.

- Cut 3 strips 6½″ × WOF, subcut into 30 rectangles 6½″ × 3½″ for Cross block.

- Cut 3 strips 12½″ × WOF, subcut into 30 rectangles 12½″ × 3½″ for Cross block.

- Cut 7 strips 2″ × WOF, piece end to end, subcut into 2 side inner borders 72½″ × 2″ and 2 top and bottom borders 63½″ × 2″. (Wait to cut until quilt top is made and measured.)

Dark gray

- Cut 4 strips 2½″ × WOF for Cross block.

- Cut 3 strips 2″ × WOF, subcut into 60 squares 2″ × 2″ for Star block.

Beige

- Outer border

  Cut 8 strips 4½″ × WOF, sew strips lengthwise together in pairs. Subcut into 2 side borders 4½″ × 75½″ and 2 top and bottom borders 4½″ × 71½″. (Wait to cut until quilt top is made and measured.)

Binding

- Cut 9 strips 2½″ × WOF.

Making the Star Block

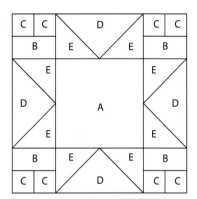

Block Diagram

A: 6½″ × 6½″   D: 7¼″ × 7¼″
B: 2″ × 3½″   E: 4″ × 4″
C: 2″ × 2″

Flying Geese Units

1. Draw a diagonal line on the wrong side of a set of 4″ star point squares.

2. Align 2 marked star-point squares to opposite corners of a 7¼″ cream square, RST. The 2 drawn lines merge into 1 continuous line from corner to corner Sew a scant ¼″ seam on both sides of the continuous line. **A**

3. Cut on the drawn line to make 2 dog-ear units. Press.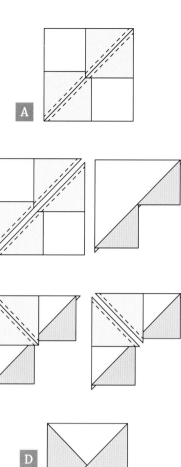

4. Align 1 star-point square to the cream corner of a dog-ear unit. Note that the marked line sits between the dog-ears. Sew a scant ¼″ seam on each side of the drawn line. Cut apart on the line to make 2 flying Geese units. Press toward the star points. Repeat with the second dog-ear unit for a total of 4 Flying Geese units.

5. Square up each Flying Geese unit to 6½″ × 3½″.

6. Repeat steps 1–4 to make 15 sets of 4 matching Flying Geese units.

> ....
> **TIP** Use a rotating cutting mat to help the squaring up process. You can also buy specific rulers for Flying Geese to make cutting a snap.

Making the Star Corners

1. Place a 2″ cream squares and a 2″ dark gray squares RST. Sew together. Repeat to make 60 units.

2. Sew a cream/dark gray unit to a cream rectangle 3½″ × 2″. Repeat to make 30 corner units with the dark gray in the right corner and 30 corner units with the dark gray in the left corner.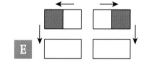

Sewing the Block

1. Lay out the quilt block units, including the matching fat eighth 6½″ square.

2. Sew the block together in rows. Press.

3. Sew the rows together. Press. The quilt block is 12½″ × 12½″ at this point.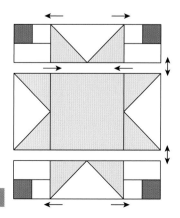

4. Repeat to make 15 Star Blocks.

Making the Cross Block

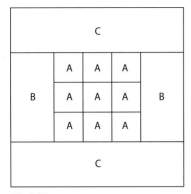

Block Diagram
A: 2½″ × 2½″ • B: 3½″ × 6½″ • C: 3½″ × 12½″

1. Sew a cream 2½″ × WOF strip to both sides of a dark gray 2½″ × WOF strip. Press. Repeat to make 2 strip sets. Cut each strip set at 2½″ increments to make 30 units.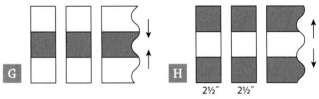

2. Sew a gray strip to both sides of a cream strip. Press. Make 1 strip set. Cut at 2½″ increments to make 15 units.

3. Make checkerboard units by sewing 3 of the units together. Press.

4. Make 15 checkerboard units.

5. Sew a cream 3½″ × 6½″ rectangle to both sides of the Cross Block. Press.

6. Sew a cream 3½″ × 12½″ rectangle to the top and bottom of the Cross Block. Press.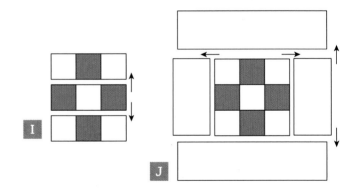

7. Make 15 Cross Blocks.

Assembling the Quilt

1. Lay out the Star Blocks and Cross Blocks, alternating them in 6 rows of 5 blocks each.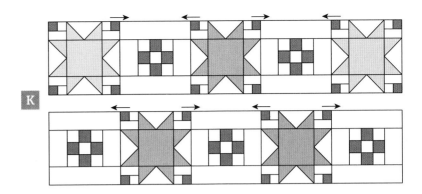

2. Sew the blocks together in rows. Press.

3. Sew the rows together. Press the seams open.

4. Sew the side inner borders onto each side of the quilt. Press.

5. Sew the top and bottom inner borders to the top and bottom of the quilt. Press.

6. Sew the side outer borders onto each side of the quilt. Press.

7. Sew the top and bottom outer borders to the top and bottom of the quilt. Press toward the borders.

Finishing

For more details, see Finishing (page 109).

1. Baste the quilt backing, batting, and quilt top together. Hand or machine quilt as desired. This quilt was machine quilted with a wicker design.

2. Make the binding and attach it to the quilt.

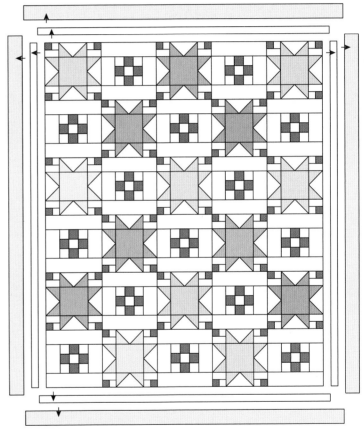

Quilt Assembly

TIP Don't be fooled by this neutral palette. The fabrics in this design could easily be switched out for Christmas, Halloween, or the 4th of July! Use the large star blocks to bring focus to your favorite fabrics!

nine lives

I am a crazy cat lady and I'm not afraid to own it! I love all things cat: clothes, home décor, fabric, and of course quilt patterns! This quilt is a fun way to show off your cat obsession. Inspired by the nine lives of cats, there are nine cat blocks in this quilt. A fun scallop border around each block makes them stand out. You can customize the blocks to any color you want.

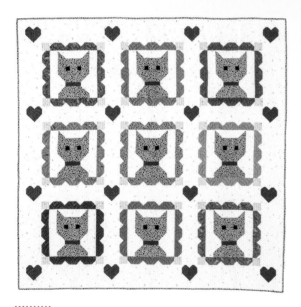

materials

FAT EIGHTHS:

9 leopard print (1 fat eighth per cat)

9 in a variety of greens for block borders

FAT QUARTERS:

1 light pink for block corners

1 magenta for hearts

10˝ × 10˝ PRECUT SQUARES:

1 magenta for collars

1 black for eyes

WHITE: 3¾ yards for blocks and borders

BINDING: ¾ yard

BACKING: 4½ yards

TIP Since each cat uses a fat eighth, it's easy to switch out the colors to customize to your feline preferences. Consider changing the cat's fur and collar to match your cat! Or use bright colors for each cat to make it more whimsical.

*Fabrics r
by Amanda Niede*

cutting

Fat eighths

- From each of 9 leopard fat eighths, cut:

  3 rectangles 2½″ × 8½″

  4 squares 2½″ × 2½″

  2 squares 1½″ × 1½″

  2 rectangle 1½″ × 4½″

  1 rectangle 1½″ × 2½″

- From each of the 9 green fat eighths, cut 2 strips 4½″ × width of fat eighth, subcut into 12 rectangles 2½″ × 4½″.

Fat quarters

- From the light pink fat quarter, cut 5 strips 2½″ × WOFQ, subcut into 36 squares 2½″ × 2½″.

- From the magenta fat quarter, cut 4 strips 4½″ × WOFQ, subcut into 32 rectangles 2½″ × 4½″ for hearts.

10″ × 10″ precut squares

- From the magenta square, cut 9 rectangles 1½″ × 4½″ for collars.

- From the black square, cut 18 squares 1½″ × 1½″ for eyes.

White

- For the Cat block, cut:

  3 strips 2½″ × WOF, subcut into 9 rectangles 2½″ × 8½″

  3 strips 2½″ × WOF, subcut into 36 squares 2½″ × 2½″

  1 strip 1½″ × WOF, subcut into 18 squares 1½″ × 1½″

  1 strip 12½″ × WOF, subcut into 16 rectangles 2½″ × 12½″

  1 strip 2½″ × WOF, subcut into 2 rectangles 2½″ × 12½″

- For the Heart block, cut:

  2 strips 1¼″ × WOF, subcut into 64 squares 1¼″ × 1¼″

  2 strips 2½″ × WOF, subcut into 32 squares 2½″ × 2½″

- For the block borders, cut 8 strips 1½″ × WOF, subcut into 216 squares 1½″ × 1½″

- For the sashing, cut 3 strips 16½″ × WOF, subcut into 24 rectangles 4½″ × 16½″

- For the border, cut 8 strips 2½″ × WOF, sew strips lengthwise together in pairs. Subcut into 2 side borders 64½″ × 2½″ and 2 top and bottom borders 68½″ × 2½″. (Wait to cut until quilt top is made and measured.)

Binding

- Cut 7 strips 2½″ × WOF.

Making the Cat Block

All seams are ¼″ unless otherwise noted. Follow the pressing arrows shown in the illustrations.

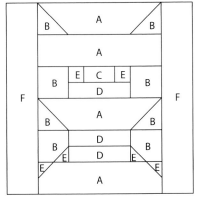

Block Diagram

A: 2½″ × 8½″   D: 1½″ × 4½″
B: 2½″ × 2½″   E: 1½″ × 1½″
C: 2½″ × 1½″   F: 2½″ × 12½″

1. To make the cat ear unit, draw a diagonal line on the WS of 2 leopard print 2½″ squares. Position the leopard squares RST with a background rectangle 2½″ × 8½″. Align the right and left corners. **A**

2. Sew on the diagonal line. Trim ¼″ away from the seam. Press. Repeat with the other square. **B**

3. To make the cat eye unit, sew a black 1½″ square to both sides of a leopard rectangle 1½″ × 2½″. Press. **C**

4. Join the eye unit to a leopard rectangle 1½″ × 4½″. **D**

5. Sew a leopard square 2½″ to both sides of the eye unit. Press. **E**

6. To make the cat chin, draw a diagonal line on the WS of 2 background 2½″ squares. Position the squares RST on both ends of the leopard rectangle 2½″ × 8½″. **F**

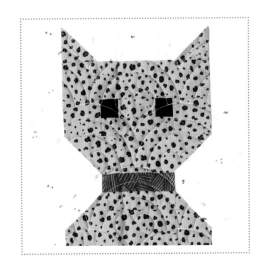

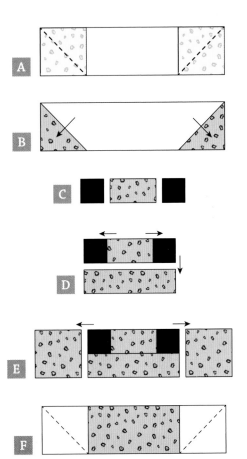

7. Sew on the diagonal line. Trim ¼˝ away from the seam. Press. **G**

8. To make the collar unit, sew a magenta rectangle 1½˝ × 4½˝ and a leopard rectangle 1½˝ × 4½˝ along the long edge. Press. **H**

9. To make the cat shoulders, draw a diagonal line on the WS of a leopard 1½˝ square. Position the leopard square on the bottom corner of a 2½˝ background square.

10. Sew on the diagonal line. Trim ¼˝ away from the seam. Press. Repeat to make a 2nd square. **I**

11. Sew a square unit to both sides of the collar unit. Press. **J**

12. Lay out all the cat units to form a cat block. Sew together. Press. **K**

13. Sew a background rectangle 2½˝ × 12½˝ to both sides of the cat block. Press. **L**

14. Repeat to make 9 total Cat blocks.

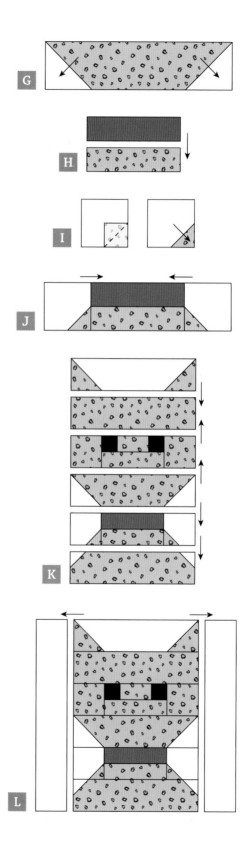

Making the Scallop Border

1. Position a background 1½˝ square RST on the top right and left corners of each green rectangle 2½˝ × 4½˝.

2. Sew on the diagonal line. Trim ¼˝ away from the seam. Press. Repeat with each of the green rectangles. **M**

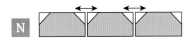

3. Sew 3 matching green rectangle units together. Repeat to make 36 scallop border units. **N**

4. Each Cat block will have 4 matching border units of 3 rectangles. Sew a pink 2½˝ square to both ends of 2 of the border units to make the top and bottom borders. **O**

5. Sew the side border units onto the Cat block. Press.

6. Sew a top and bottom border unit onto the Cat block. Press.

7. Repeat steps 4–6, adding a border to each of the 9 cat blocks. **P**

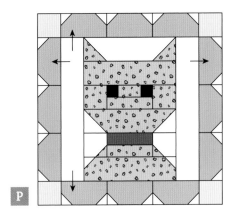

Making the Heart Blocks

1. Draw a diagonal line on the wrong side of the background 1¼˝ squares. Position a background 1¼˝ square RST on both top corners of a magenta 2½˝ × 4½˝ rectangle.

2. Sew on the diagonal line. Trim ¼˝ away from the seam. Press.

3. Draw a diagonal line on the wrong side of the background 2½˝ squares. Align the square RST with the bottom edge of a rectangle.

4. Sew on the diagonal line. Trim ¼˝ away from the seam. Press. **Q**

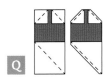

5. Repeat with the opposite side of the heart. Make sure the bottom angles form a "V". **R**

6. Sew the right side and the left side of the heart together. Press the seam open. The block will measure 4½˝ × 4½˝ at this point. **S**

7. Repeat to make 16 Heart blocks.

Assembling the Quilt

1. To make a sashing row, sew 4 Heart blocks between and at each end of 3 sashing rectangles 16½″ × 4½″. Make 4 sashing rows.

2. To make a block row, sew 4 sashing rectangles 16½″ × 4½″ between and at each end of 3 blocks. Press. Make 3 block rows.

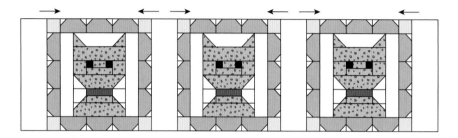

3. Sew the quilt together in rows, alternating the sashing rows and block rows.

4. Sew the side borders to the quilt front and press.

5. Sew the top and bottom borders to the quilt front and press.

Finishing

For more details, see Finishing (page 109).

1. Baste the quilt backing, batting, and quilt top together. Hand or machine quilt as desired. This quilt was machine quilted with a rainbow heart design.

2. Make the binding and attach it to the quilt.

> **TIP** Since all the blocks in this book are the same size you can switch out the cat blocks and use this pattern to frame any block of your choosing.

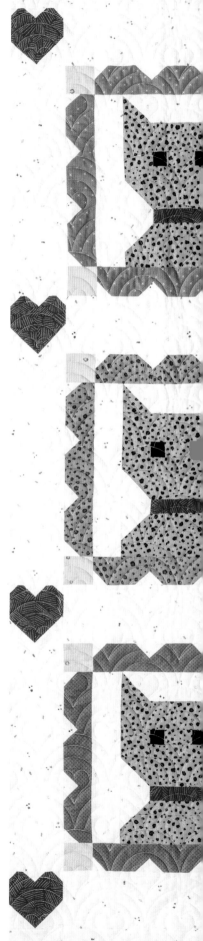

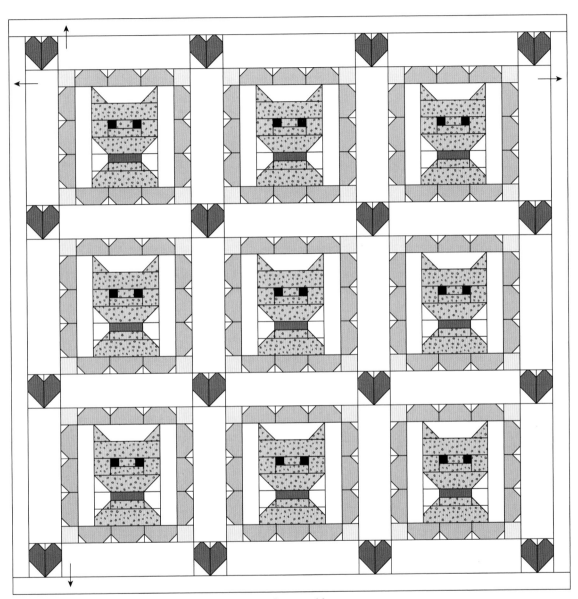

Quilt Assembly

four-block
table runner

Table runners are a fun way to add a quilty touch to your home. Of course you can put a table runner on a table, but you can also put one on a dresser, night stand, ottoman, hearth, towel rack, or basket. I use table runners in each of these ways! This table runner is made up of four blocks and sashing. You can choose four of the same blocks or mix it up with a variety of blocks. I used the Mod Diamonds block (page 20) for this table runner.

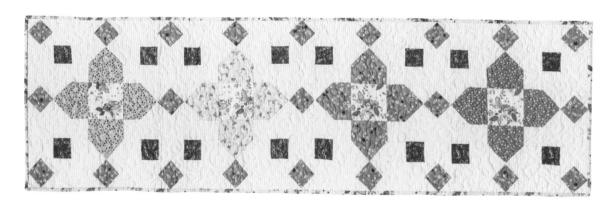

materials

BLOCKS: 4 finished blocks from this book

FAT QUARTER: 1 gold

WHITE: ¾ yard

BINDING: ½ yard

BACKING: 1¼ yards

cutting

Fat Quarter

- Cut 5 strips 3½″ × WOFQ, subcut into 23 squares 3½″ × 3½″.

Background

- Cut 5 strips 2″ × WOF, subcut into 92 squares 2″ × 2″.

- Cut 4 strips 3½″ × WOF, subcut into 26 rectangles 3½″ × 5″.

Binding

- Cut 5 strips 2½″ × WOF.

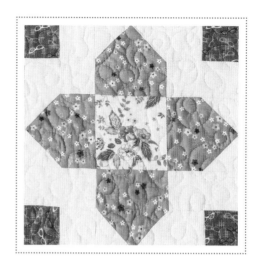

Making the Table Runner

All seams are ¼″ unless otherwise noted. Follow the pressing arrows shown in the illustrations.

1. Make 4 blocks according to the instructions in the book. All the blocks are 12½″ before they are set in a quilt.

2. Draw a diagonal line on the wrong side of the white 2″ squares. Place a white square RST on the top corner of a gold 3½″ square.

3. Sew on the diagonal line. Trim ¼″ away from the seam. Press. **A**

4. Repeat with the other 3 corners. **B**

5. Repeat to make 23 diamonds.

6. Using a diamond block, sew a 5″ × 3½″ white rectangle to both sides of the diamond block forming a sashing unit. Press. **C**

7. Repeat step 6 to make 13 sashing units.

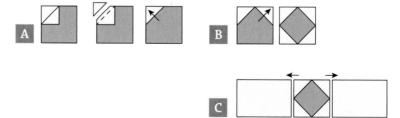

8. Sew a sashing unit between and at each end of 4 blocks. Press.

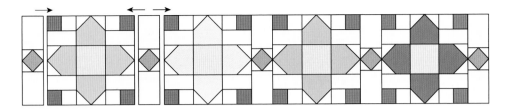

9. To make a sashing row, sew 5 diamond blocks between and at each end of 4 sashing units. Press. Repeat to make 2.

10. Sew the sashing rows to the top and bottom of the block row. Press seams open.

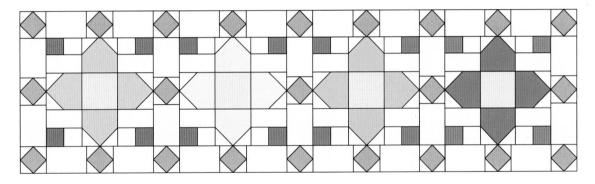

Finishing

For more details, see Finishing (page 109).

1. Baste the quilt backing, batting, and quilt top together. Hand or machine quilt as desired. This quilt was machine quilted with a loopy design.

2. Make the binding and attach it to the quilt.

nine-square quilt

I learned how to quilt by making baby quilts. They are such fun quilt projects. They don't require a ton of yardage or time. This quilt uses nine blocks with some clever sashing. You can choose any blocks from this book. I am using the Cross block from Woodland Christmas (page 64). It's fun to see how different blocks can look by just changing up the colors.

materials

BLOCKS: 9 finished blocks from this book

AQUA: ½ yard

GOLD: ¼ yard

WHITE: 1¼ yards

BINDING: ½ yard

BACKING: 3½ yards

Fabric is a collection of fabrics by Lori Holt
for Riley Blake Designs.

Aqua

- Cut 1 strip 12½″ × WOF, subcut into 24 rectangles 12½″ × 1½″.

Gold

- Cut 2 strips 1½″ × WOF, subcut into 32 squares 1½″ × 1½″.

- Cut 1 strip 3½″ × WOF, subcut into 16 rectangles 3½″ × 1½″.

White

- Cut 3 strips 1½″ × WOF, subcut into 64 squares 1½″ × 1½″.

- Cut 2 strips 12½″ × WOF, subcut into 48 rectangles 12½″ × 1½″.

- Cut 6 strips 1½″ × WOF, piece end to end, subcut into 2 side borders 48½″ × 1½″ and 2 top and bottom borders 50½″ × 1½″. (Wait to cut until quilt top is made and measured.)

Binding

- Cut 6 strips 2½″ × WOF.

Making the Baby Quilt

1. Make 9 of the Cross Blocks from Woodland Christmas (page 64).

2. To make the sashing units, gather the white and aqua 12½″ × 1½″ rectangles.

Sew a white rectangle 12½″ × 1½″ to both sides of an aqua rectangle 12½″ × 1½″. Press. **A**

3. Repeat step 2 to make 24 sashing units.

4. For the Plus corner blocks, sew a white 1½″ square on either side of a gold 1½″ square. Repeat to make a second unit. Sew a white/gold/white unit to the top and bottom of a gold rectangle 3½″ × 1½″. Press. **B**

5. Repeat step 4 to make 16 Plus corner blocks.

6. To make a sashing row, sew 4 Plus blocks between and at each end of three rectangle sashing units. Press. Repeat to make 4 sashing rows. **C**

7. To make the block row, sew a rectangle sashing unit in between and at each end of 3 blocks. Press. Repeat to make 3 block rows. **D**

8. Sew the quilt together in rows, alternating the sashing and the block rows. Press.

9. Sew the side borders to the quilt front. Sew the top and bottom borders to the quilt front. Press toward the borders.

Finishing

For more details, see Finishing (page 109).

1. Baste the quilt backing, batting, and quilt top together. Hand or machine quilt as desired. This quilt was machine quilted with an oleander design.

2. Make the binding and attach it to the quilt.

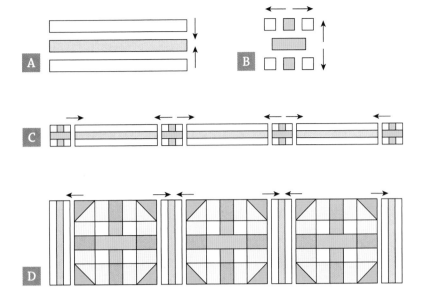

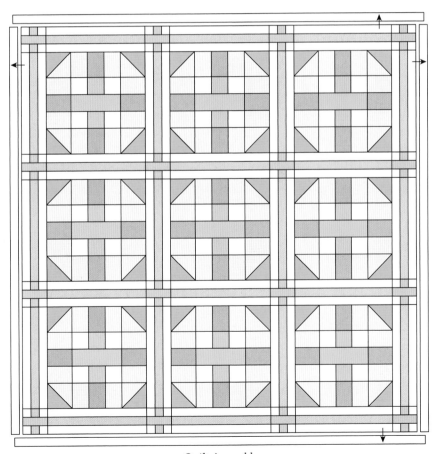

Quilt Assembly

one-patch pillow

Throw pillows are my favorite way to decorate my house for seasons and holidays. All my pillows use 20″ pillow forms which makes switching the pillow covers out a snap. Also, storing pillow covers is easy since they fold nicely and lay flat! This pillow is a fun way to use one block from the book. Simply choose your favorite block and follow the instructions for the borders.

materials

BLOCK: 1 finished block from this book

RED: 16 scraps in a variety of prints

BLUE: 16 scraps in a variety of prints

WHITE: ¼ yard

PILLOW BACKING: ⅔ yard

BATTING: 22″ × 22″

BINDING: ¼ yard

TIP Use a variety of blues and reds to make the pillow more interesting.

Fabric is an assortment of fabrics by Riley Blake Designs.

Red

• Cut 16 red squares
2½″ × 2½″.

Blue

• Cut 16 blue squares
2½″ × 2½″.

White

• Cut 1 strip 1½″ × WOF,
subcut 2 inner side borders
1½″ × 12½″.

• Cut 1 strip 1½″ × WOF,
subcut 2 inner top and
bottom borders 1½″ × 14½″.

• Cut 1 strip 1½″ × WOF,
subcut 2 outer side borders
1½″ × 18½″.

• Cut 1 strip 1½″ × WOF,
subcut 2 outer top and
bottom borders 1½″ × 20½″.

Binding

• Cut 3 strips 2½″ × 2½″.

Making the Pillow

1. Make any block from this book for the center. This pillow uses the Playful Pinwheel block (page 26).

2. Sew the red and blue squares together as shown in the diagram. Make 2 of each.

Press in one direction.

Make 2 side borders.

Make 2 top and bottom borders.

3. Sew the white inner side borders to the block. Press.

4. Sew the white inner top and bottom borders onto the block. Press. **A**

5. Sew the side patchwork borders to both sides of the pillow front. Press.

6. Sew the top and bottom patchwork borders onto the pillow front. Press. **B**

7. Sew the white outer side borders onto the pillow front. Press.

8. Sew the white top and bottom borders onto the pillow front. Press. **C**

9. Now that the pillow top is complete, baste it with batting and quilt it. I quilted a simple diagonal grid pattern. **D**

10. Finish the pillow in your favorite method: envelope back or zippered back.

Adding Binding

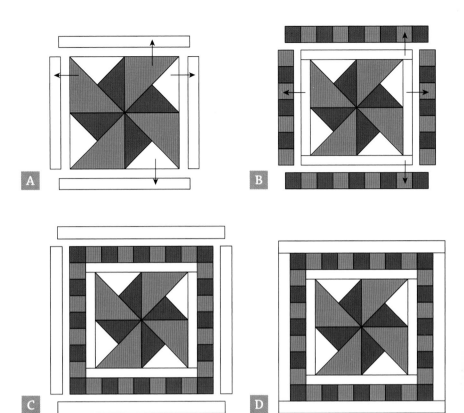

For a fun binding trim, don't sew and turn the pillow top and pillow back. Instead, layer the pillow top and pillow back WST. Sew a ⅛″ seam around the whole pillow. Attach binding to the pillow just as you would a quilt and hand sew on the back. It's an easy way to get a "piping" effect.

....
> **TIP** You don't have to make this into a pillow. Simply quilt the top and bind it and you have a 20″ × 20″ mini quilt!

General Instructions

Backing and Batting

Backing

There are several choices of fabric when it comes to quilt backing. Most often I use quilting cotton that coordinates with my quilt top. You can also piece quilting fabric together in large sections, add an accent row, or even quilt blocks to your quilt back. If I know the quilt is going to be a "snuggle on the couch" quilt, I put minky on the back. We have a stack of quilts in the family room with minky backs, and they are our favorites! Flannel is another good choice for a soft and cozy back—just make sure you prewash and dry the flannel before using it to ensure that it doesn't shrink after quilting. One last quilt back option is to use a high-quality cotton bedsheet. I used a vintage sheet on the back of one quilt. So cute!

Preparing the Backing

Plan on cutting or making the quilt backing at least 8″ longer and 8″ wider than the quilt top. Most often this will involve piecing the fabric.

Here is my quick formula to decide how much fabric you will need.

If the quilt top is between 34″ and 74″ in length:

1. Add 8″ to the width of the quilt top, divide this number by 36, and then multiply it by 2. This number indicates the total yardage needed.

2. Cut the yardage in half widthwise. Sew the 2 pieces right sides together using a ½″ seam along the selvages. Trim the seam down to ¼″.

If the quilt top is longer than 74″ in length:

1. Add 8″ to the width of the quilt top, divide this number by 36, and then multiply it by 3. This number indicates total yardage needed.

2. Cut the yardage widthwise in 3 equal lengths (in thirds). Sew the selvages right sides together using a ½″ seam to create one piece of fabric with 3 equal-size sections. Trim the seams down to ¼″.

Batting

Typically batting is sold in widths wide enough that you don't have to piece the batting, like you do the backing fabric. Most battings are 60″, 96″, or 120″ wide.

The variety of battings available is simply amazing. It can almost be overwhelming. I have narrowed my batting preference down to the following two types.

• Heirloom Premium 80/20 Cotton/Poly Blend (by Hobbs Bonded Fibers) offers more loft and less weight than traditional cotton batting. It is durable and machine washable. This batting is made with a blend of 80% natural cotton and 20% fine polyester, is needle punched, and has a light resin bonding to provide exceptional strength and durability. Close quilting yields a flat, low-loft appearance, while more space between stitching lines yields a slightly higher loft.

• I also use Hobbs Tuscany Cotton Wool Batting. It is a blend of 80% fine cotton and 20% superwashed wool. The wool adds loft, which gives greater detail to the stitching pattern and reduces crease marks from settling into quilts. The wool also adds additional warmth which I love!

TIP If you quilt a lot, you end up with a stack of batting scraps. Don't throw them away! You can piece batting together. Make sure the edges of the batting are cut straight and are not crooked. Then, using a large zigzag stitch, push the edges of the batting together and zigzag stitch so the stitch catches both pieces of batting. This allows the batting to lie flat, and the quilting reinforces the batting seam.

Quilt Basics

Before you begin your quilt make sure to read these quilt basics and techniques.

Seam Allowances

A ¼″ seam allowance is used for most projects. It's a good idea to do a test seam before you begin sewing to check that your ¼″ is accurate. Accuracy is the key to successful piecing.

There is no need to backstitch. Seam Lines will be crossed by another seam, which will anchor them.

Pressing

Press all seams as indicated in the instructions and as directed by the arrows in the diagrams. Seams will be either pressed to one side or pressed open. For easier open seam pressing, press seams to one side first, then press seams open. Use an up and down motion to avoid distorting the fabric. Be especially careful when pressing bias edges as they stretch easily.

Stitch and Flip Method

This method lets you use triangles in your quilting without having to actually cut triangles. Let's use the example of this sashing square from Summer Meadow (page 40).

The pink square is cut 3½″ × 3½″ and the white squares are cut 1½″ × 1½″. Draw a diagonal line on the back of the white squares. Position a white square RST on a corner of the pink square. Sew on the diagonal line. Trim ¼″ away from the seam. "Flip" the newly formed triangle over and press. By repeating this method with each corner, you now have a snowball style block with triangle corners without ever cutting a triangle.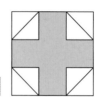

Half-Square Triangles (HST)

Half-square triangles are featured frequently throughout this book. They are used to create different geometric patterns and are very simple to make. There are two ways to make them. One method produces two half-square triangles that need to be squared up after pressing; the other method produces one half-square triangle, but it doesn't need to be squared up.

Making Two Half-Square Triangles

Sew ¼″ away from both sides of the diagonal line to yield 2 half-square triangles.

1. Start with 2 same-size, different-color squares.

2. Draw a diagonal line on the wrong side of one square.

3. Place the 2 squares RST and sew ¼″ away from both sides of the diagonal line.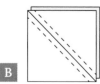

4. Cut on the diagonal line, yielding 2 HSTs. Press open.

5. Square up each HST to the desired size.

Making One Half-Square Triangle

Sew on the diagonal line to yield 1 half-square triangle.

1. Draw a diagonal line on the wrong side of one square.

2. Place 2 same-size, different-color squares RST.

3. Sew directly on the diagonal line.

4. Trim the seam allowance to ¼″.

5. Press the seam open. Discard the scraps.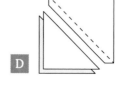

Finishing

Instructions for basting, quilting, and binding are provided in this section.

Layering

Spread the pressed backing wrong side up and tape the edges to a flat surface with masking tape. (If you are working on carpet, you can use T-pins to secure the backing to the carpet.) Center the batting on top, smoothing out any folds. Place the quilt top right side up on top of the batting and backing, making sure it is centered. This is often referred to as the *quilt sandwich*.

Photo by Lauren Herberg for C&T Photography

Basting

Basting keeps the quilt sandwich layers from shifting while you are quilting.

If you plan to machine quilt, *pin baste* the quilt layers together with safety pins placed about 3″–4″ apart. Begin placing the pins in the center and move toward the edges, first in vertical and then horizontal rows. Try not to pin directly on the intended quilting lines.

As an alternative to pinning, try using a basting spray (like SpraynBond) to hold the layers together. The spray is temporary and washes out. It holds all the layers of the quilt sandwich together without pins. Spray the wrong side of the quilt back and lay the batting on top, smoothing any wrinkles. Then spray the batting and lay the quilt top on top, smoothing the wrinkles.

Quilting

Quilting, whether by hand or machine, enhances the pieced or appliquéd design of the quilt. You may choose to quilt-in-the-ditch, echo the pieced designs, use patterns from quilting design books and stencils, or do your own free-motion quilting.

Binding the Quilt

The binding for all projects in this book is 2½″ wide.

1. Prepare the binding by sewing 2½″ strips together using diagonal seams until you reach the necessary length. **E–F**

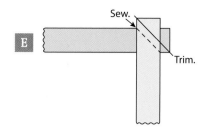

2. Trim the seam allowances and press the seams open to reduce bulk. Press the binding in half lengthwise, wrong sides together.

3. Starting in the middle of one side of the quilt, line up the raw edges of the binding with the raw edge of the quilt. Skipping the first 8″ of the binding, use a ¼″ seam allowance to stitch the binding to the quilt. Stop ¼″ away from the first corner and backstitch 1 stitch. **G**

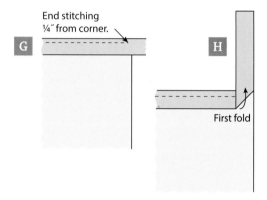

4. Lift the presser foot and needle. Rotate the quilt one-quarter turn. Fold the binding at a right angle so it extends straight above the quilt and the fold forms a 45° angle in the corner. **H**

5. Bring the binding strip down even with the edge of the quilt. Begin sewing at the folded edge. Repeat in the same manner at all corners. **I**

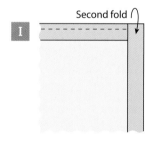

6. Once you have pivoted at all corners, keep sewing until you have 12″ left to reach the beginning stitches. Trim the tails of each end of the binding to overlap by exactly 2½″. Unfold the binding tails and bring them right sides together, matching the edges, as shown. Mark a diagonal line as indicated. Sew along the marked line, trim the ¼″ seam, and press the seam open. **J**

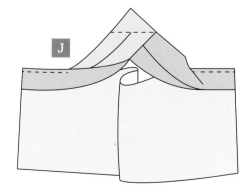

7. Fold the binding back in half and pin in place onto the quilt top (it should be an exact fit). You can give it a little press with the iron to make it lie nicely. Finish stitching the binding in place.

8. Bring the folded edge of the binding up and over to the back of the quilt. Pin in place and miter the corners. Hand stitch the binding in place.

About the Author

Amanda Niederhauser grew up at the side of her mother's sewing machine, playing with buttons, spools, and zippers. As a child and teenager she would sew pillows, shorts, scrunchies, and stuffed cats. It wasn't until she graduated college and moved to Virginia that quilting became her first love.

It was through trial and error that she taught herself to quilt. She would often see a quilt and recreate it as there was no YouTube, Instagram, or Internet. This early training of making up quilt patterns helped her develop a love for quilt design and pattern making. Amanda turned her love for pattern design into a love for fabric design and designs fabric for Riley Blake Designs.

Most days Amanda can be found at her Southern California home in her sewing studio with her cat, Mufasa. Amanda has an extremely patient husband, David, and three adorable children, Ella, Ryan, and Sally.

About the Author's Cat

Mufasa, the Bengal cat, is the head of quality control, chief quilt inspector, and A list quilt model. Mufasa has his paws on every quilt that comes out of Amanda's sewing studio. His favorite napping place is on a quilt or in the middle of the cutting table. He is extremely helpful and devoted to all things quilting.

CREATIVE SPARK
ONLINE LEARNING

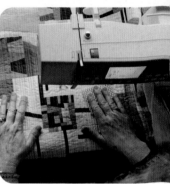

Quilting courses to become an expert quilter...

From their studio to yours, Creative Spark instructors are teaching you how to create and become a master of your craft. So not only do you get a look inside their creative space, you also get to be a part of engaging courses that would typically be a one or multi-day workshop from the comfort of your home.

Creative Spark is not your one-size-fits-all online learning experience. We welcome you to be who you are, share, create, and belong.

Scan for a gift from us!

creativespark.ctpub.com